P9-DIY-207

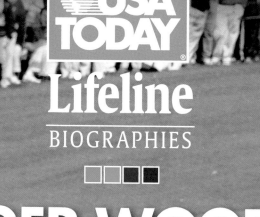

TIGER WOODS
Golf's Master

by Jeremy Roberts

Twenty-First Century Books · Minneapolis

CHESTERFIELD COUNTY LIBRARY
VIRGINIA

USA TODAY®, its logo, and associated graphics are federally registered trademarks. All rights are reserved. All USA TODAY text, graphic and photographs are used pursuant to a license and may not be reproduced, distributed or otherwise used without the express written consent of Gannett Co., Inc.

Photos and graphics on pp. 1, 11, 16 (bottom right), 28, 32, 45, 50, 51 (top right), 51 (bottom), 54, 58, 69 (both), 73, 74, 75, 76, 79, 80, 82, 86, 88, 89, 91, 95, 98 (both), 99 (both), 100, 101, all backgrounds © copyright 2009 by USA TODAY
USA TODAY Snapshots® and excerpts from USA TODAY articles quoted on back cover and on pages 32, 42, 45, 54–55, 68, 69, 71, 76–77, 77, 81, 89, 92, 95 © copyright 2009 by USA TODAY

Copyright © 2009 by Jim DeFelice

All rights reserved. International copyright secured. No part of this book may be reproduced, stored in a retrieval system, or transmitted in any form or by any means—electronic, mechanical, photocopying, recording, or otherwise—without the prior written permission of Lerner Publishing Group, Inc., except for the inclusion of brief quotations in an acknowledged review.

Twenty-First Century Books
A division of Lerner Publishing Group, Inc.
241 First Avenue North
Minneapolis, MN 55401 U.S.A.

Website address: www.lernerbooks.com

The publisher wishes to thank Richard Curtis, Jerry Potter, Monte Lorell, Julie Snider, and Ben Nussbaum of USA TODAY for their help in preparing this book.

Library of Congress Cataloging-in-Publication Data

Roberts, Jeremy, 1956–
    Tiger Woods: golf's master / by Jeremy Roberts
        p.m.   c.m. — (Lifeline biographies)
    Includes bibliographical references and index.
    ISBN 978–1–58013–569–6 (lib. bdg. : alk. paper)
    1. Woods, Tiger—Juvenile literature. 2. Golfers—United States—Biography—Juvenile literature. I. Title
    GV964.352092—dc22   2008003098

Manufactured in the United States of America
1 2 3 4 5 6 – PA – 14 13 12 11 10 09

Baby steps: Toddler Tiger Woods sizes up his putt at the Navy Golf Course near his home in California.

A Genius

The little boy slipped down from the high chair, toddling toward his father in the garage of their California home. His dad looked over in amazement as the nine-month-old picked up the golf club he had received as a toy. Father and son had spent many sessions in the garage these past three months. Dad would launch practice shots into a net as the baby watched.

Usually the little boy just cooed and smiled. But on this day, the baby picked up the small golf club. Then, on unsteady feet, the toddler approached one of the balls on the practice carpet. He pulled his golf club back, waved it slightly as his daddy had, and swung like an expert. The ball flew into the net. "We have a genius on our hands!" the excited father told his wife after that swing.

Perhaps it was a lucky shot. Perhaps it was fate. Perhaps over time that first swing has come to seem better than it really was. But no matter—the toddler's early tee shot was an omen. The child was Tiger Woods. Over the next thirty years, he would develop into the finest golfer the world has ever known.

Of course, at the time no one knew how great Tiger Woods would be. The odds against any athlete are immense. Even someone with great natural talent can be distracted or suffer misfortune. He or she will certainly be discouraged along the way. Often it is difficult to tell exactly what helps and what hurts a young person's development.

Tiger Woods faced one obstacle many golfers never encounter. Tiger's dad is mostly African American. His mother comes from Thailand. While American society has changed greatly since the civil rights battles of the 1950s and

Lots of support: The close relationship Tiger *(left)* has had with his parents has been key to his long-term success.

1960s, prejudice remains. This is true in sports, despite the efforts and achievements of many.

By the time Tiger picked up his golf club, African American stars were common in baseball, basketball, and football. However, golf had never had an African American superstar. Relatively few African Americans played professional golf. In fact, in many places, African Americans were still openly discouraged from playing the game, even for recreation.

But prejudice would not hold back Tiger Woods. With talent, hard work, and a great deal of love and support from his parents, he overcame the odds to become one of the greatest athletes of all time. And he keeps getting better.

Green Beret: Green Berets help a wounded South Vietnamese soldier. Earl Woods was part of this U.S. Army group, which was training the South Vietnamese army to fully take over defense of South Vietnam against its North Vietnamese opponent.

Tiger Cub

Major Earl Woods leaned back in the bamboo thicket. A sniper had just missed killing him. Woods decided he needed a few minutes of quiet. But this was Vietnam. The country had been at war for nearly three decades. No place was ever really safe, especially in the early 1970s.

"Woody!" yelled a voice. "Don't move!"

Woods didn't.

"There's a bamboo viper about two inches from your right eye," said South Vietnamese army colonel Vuong Dang Phong. Phong coaxed his friend to keep still for several more minutes as one of the most dangerous snakes in the world slid a few inches from his face. One wrong move— even a hiccup or a sneeze—and the snake could have seriously injured or killed Woods and Phong. Finally, the snake slipped away. Woods beat a quick retreat.

It was neither the first nor last time that the two men faced danger together. Major Woods was an excellent soldier and would earn a special medal for his bravery, but it was Phong he considered special. He began calling the Vietnamese colonel Tiger. The nickname was a tribute to Phong's bravery.

Earl Woods was in Vietnam in 1970 for his second assignment in the war-torn country. By then, U.S. troops had been in South Vietnam for many years, trying to help the government in its fight against the Communist North Vietnamese. Woods was a Green Beret major. His job was to help the South Vietnamese improve their army so they could defend themselves better. The war was not very popular in the United States, but soldiers like Earl Woods believed that their fight would help keep Communism from spreading.

Woods soon went home. The United States eventually withdrew all of its troops. South Vietnam was defeated by North Vietnam. But Earl Woods would never forget the man who saved his life.

Eldrick "Tiger" Woods

By 1974 Earl Woods, who had been promoted to lieutenant colonel, was ready to retire from the army and rejoin civilian life. He had married a woman from Thailand named Kultida Punswad in 1973 and wanted to settle down with her in the United States. Kultida— often called Tida by family and friends—had met Earl when he was stationed in Bangkok a few years earlier. They had fallen in love almost immediately. Kultida became Earl's second wife. (Earl and his first wife were divorced. They had two sons and a daughter.)

A few months before Earl left the army, another officer introduced him to golf. In a few months, Earl became a fanatic. Very competitive

Bangkok, Thailand: Earl Woods met his wife Kultida in Bangkok, the capital of Thailand.

by nature, he spent hours and hours practicing, determined to beat his friend. Finally, he challenged him to a match—and won. Earl continued to hone his game after taking a job as a contracts administrator with McDonnell Douglas, a large company in California.

 Tiger's half brothers are Earl Jr. (born 1955) and Kevin (born 1957). His half sister, Royce, was born in 1958.

He was still improving when his new son was born on December 30, 1975. The boy was named Eldrick, a unique name that begins with his father's first initial and ends with his mother's. Kultida said that she gave him that name so that he would be surrounded by both parents throughout his life. Right from the start, Earl called the infant Tiger, in honor of the man who had saved his life in Vietnam.

A Natural

Both Kultida and Earl doted on their son. According to Earl, Kultida's Asian background played an important role in shaping Tiger.

IN F⊕CUS

Golf Basics

The object of golf is very simple—using a club, hit a small ball into a small hole. Learning the basics doesn't take long. Perfecting them can take a lifetime.

Golfers score a point, or stroke, each time they hit the ball. The goal is to score the fewest number of strokes. A golfer hits the ball, waits until it stops, then hits it again until sinking it in the cup at the end of the hole. The word *hole* is used to mean both the cup and the entire playing area around and leading to the cup.

Golf courses typically have eighteen holes. One eighteen-hole session is a round. A professional tournament generally consists of four rounds. Whoever scores the lowest overall total is the winner.

Players begin by teeing off, or hitting the ball from a tee at the starting area. Their goal is the cup a few hundred yards away. The cup sits on a green, a special area with very smooth grass. Gentle shots, called putts, are used to roll the ball into the hole.

Between the starting area and the green is a long fairway, which has short grass where the ball can be easily hit. Slightly higher grass known as the rough is generally located on either side of the fairway. Golfers usually find it a little harder to hit a ball

"The way Tiger was taught to respect his parents and other adults, to rely on his instincts and feelings, to be unselfish and generous," said Earl, "these are all tenets of Asian philosophy and culture that he has embraced."

Tiger also embraced golf, which he began "studying" in the garage at about six months old. His father had no intention of teaching the infant the game so early. His father just brought him along while he practiced.

Small children rarely have much upper-body strength or coordination. Both are important in golf, especially when driving, or hitting

from the rough because of the height of the grass and nearby obstacles, such as trees.

To make things even more difficult, traps, or bunkers, sit near the green. These are areas of sand or rough earth. Hitting a ball from a bunker requires a great deal of skill. The ball must be lofted from the trap just hard enough to clear the sand but not so hard as to sail into another hazard. Pools of water and large wooded areas also make things more complicated for golfers. If a ball lands in one of these areas, the golfer must hit it out or add a penalty shot to his or her score.

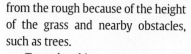

The overall design of each hole—a tee, a fairway, and a green—is the same from hole to hole and course to course. But the shape of individual holes varies greatly. The distance from tee to cup also varies. Each golf course presents different problems to the players.

When designers create a golf course, they consider each hole and determine how many shots a very good golfer would need to get the ball from the tee into the cup. This number is called par. Golfers can measure themselves against par on each hole. Par for each hole usually ranges from 3 to 5, depending on the size of the golf course.

the ball far down the fairway (the part of a golf course between the tee and the green). According to his father, Tiger displayed that natural ability from a very young age. He also quickly learned how to use different types of swings to send the ball high or far. Even before he could read, said his dad, Tiger could recognize swings well enough to say that someone had a flaw in his swing.

Smiling toddler: At eighteen months, Tiger already has the stance and the big smile of a champion.

Instead of carrying a rattle, said Earl, Tiger "had a putter." Soon after Tiger learned how to walk, he accompanied his dad to the Navy Golf Course in Los Alamitos, near their home in Cypress, California. Earl had special clubs made for Tiger and began showing him how to play. When he was about two, Tiger even memorized his father's office phone number and would call to ask if they could play golf after work. Father and son were soon regulars on the course.

In golf, competitors measure themselves against a score, called par, and try to get a lower score. Earl soon established a special scoring system to make the game more interesting for Tiger. This "Tiger par" system showed the young golfer how many shots it should take him to sink the ball in a hole.

Tiger's talents went beyond athleticism. He began memorizing multiplication tables when he was three years old. He soon mastered basic math. He seemed happy and willing to please adults who took an interest in him, and he would often demonstrate his golf prowess. He also learned to deal with attention. He had to, because word soon spread that pint-sized Tiger Woods was a golf prodigy.

Left-handed?: At first, Earl thought Tiger might be left-handed. But by the age of three, he was showing off a smooth, right-handed swing.

First Steps

Tiger Woods walked quickly from the side of the stage toward the lights. Not yet three, he didn't completely understand what was going on, but he did know one thing—he was there to hit a golf ball.

Television talk show host Mike Douglas waved him forward with a friendly grin. Douglas introduced Tiger and his dad to the audience and then helped little Tiger find the right spot on the fake golf course green at center stage. He stood back as Tiger waved his specially sized golf club. The ball sailed long and straight—a perfect drive.

Tiger wasn't done. Douglas called out one of his guests, the famous comedian Bob Hope. Hope's comedy routines and appearances often included jokes about golf. Hope aped for the camera, asking the little boy, with a wink, if he had any money to place a bet. But it was Tiger who stole the show. Challenged to a putting competition, he agreed— then grabbed his ball and plopped it down half an inch from the hole. The audience cracked up.

Prejudice

Tiger's trip to *The Mike Douglas Show* in 1978 was one of several TV appearances during his days as a preschooler and young boy. He went on such shows as *That's Incredible.* Viewers were surprised that such a young child could swing golf clubs so perfectly, especially under the glare of TV lights. People would laugh or think he was very cute. A few were impressed by his powerful and well-balanced swing. But most viewers probably thought he was just an interesting and unusual child who would eventually tire of golf and show biz.

 In 1981 five-year-old Tiger sat on the lap of football great Fran Tarkenton during *That's Incredible.* Tarkenton was the host of the show. During the show, Tiger hit Whiffle balls into the audience.

Off camera, however, Tiger's golf skills were growing. When Tiger was four, the Navy Golf Course limited his play. The officials said it was because of his age, but Earl believed it was because he and his son were African American.

Like many American sports and institutions, golf has a history of prejudice against minorities. Private clubs own many golf courses. To play at a course regularly, a person has to be a member of the club.

Driving Past Prejudice

Until the early 1970s, PGA Tour rules made it difficult for minority golfers to qualify to compete in major events. An African American did not compete at the Masters Tournament until Lee Elder made the field in 1975. But, as Tiger often points out, he was not the first African American golfer to do well.

Jim Dent was not considered a standout as a member of the PGA Tour. But as a member of the Champions Tour, a series of separate events for older golfers, Dent has been a star. Since 1989 he has taken away more than $5 million in prize money and has notched more than ten titles.

Robert Lee Elder, generally known as Lee Elder, ranks as one of the finest golfers ever. Best known as the first African American to play at the Masters, Elder won more than $1 million on the PGA Tour. Among his most memorable matches was a dramatic sudden-death playoff

against Jack Nicklaus at the American Golf Classic in 1968, Elder's first year on the Tour. Nicklaus edged him out on the fifth hole in one of the tightest showdowns Nicklaus ever faced.

Calvin Peete turned pro in the 1970s and joined the PGA Tour full-time when he was in his early thirties. Despite different ailments, including an elbow he broke as a youth, Peete managed a dozen tournament victories and twice made the prestigious Ryder Cup team, which competes internationally representing the United States. His winnings on the PGA Tour topped $2.3 million.

Charlie Sifford joined the PGA Tour in 1960. Among his victories were the Greater Hartford Open in 1967 and the Los Angeles Open in 1969. His career earnings on the PGA Tour were $341,344. He had considerable success on the PGA Champions Tour. Sifford detailed his life and struggles to overcome prejudice in the book *Just Let Me Play*.

In most cases, membership is very expensive, which keeps some minorities from joining.

Some clubs also have strict rules about who will be accepted for membership. In some cases, the rules or informal practices kept African Americans and other minorities from joining. Even when they were allowed to play, they were often discriminated against with late starting times. This sometimes meant they played their final holes in the dark. While these practices changed during the 1960s, discrimination against African Americans at golf courses and clubs continued during the late 1970s.

At the navy course, all retired military officers were allowed to play, including Earl. But rules prohibited children under ten from playing. At first, the rules did not seem to be enforced for anyone. Then suddenly, club officials cited the rules to keep Tiger out.

Earl Woods, whose ancestors included Native Americans as well as African Americans, had experienced prejudice for many years, on and off the golf course. He had encountered biased officers in the army. When the family first moved into the California neighborhood where Tiger was raised, for example, someone shot at their house with a BB gun. Sometimes members at the military golf club called Earl "Sergeant Brown," a not-so-subtle reference to the color of his skin.

"It was inconceivable to them that a black guy could rise above the rank of sergeant," said Earl. As a lieutenant colonel, he outranked many, if not all, of his detractors. He had served in an elite unit and put his life on the line in Vietnam not once but twice—extreme measures of heroism by anyone's standards. But Earl said that this didn't stop some members from disliking him and his family and trying to hurt them.

Earl had learned to deal with prejudice throughout his life, first as a college baseball player and then as an army officer. His philosophy could be summed up in one word: perseverance. Kultida had similar beliefs. Both passed this attitude on to Tiger.

IN FOCUS

Tiger's Attitude about Race

Tiger thinks of himself as a combination of many different backgrounds. He values his father's African American and Native American roots. He also feels close to his mother's Asian and European heritage. Growing up, he came to think of himself as a conglomeration of all these cultures. In fact, Tiger came up with a word to describe the mixture by combining the words *Caucasian, Black, Indian,* and *Asian.* The word was *cablinasian.* "The bottom line is that I am an American," he would tell reporters years later. "And proud of it."

Woods honors late father

Like Mozart

Rules or racial prejudice weren't about to stop the Woodses. Tiger's mother decided to find another course where he could play. She found Heartwell Golf Park, a small course in Long Beach, California, roughly fifteen miles from their home. One of the professionals at the course, whose job it was to help golfers, asked to see Tiger play.

"I was blown away," said the golf pro, Rudy Duran. "It was unbelievable. He was awesome. He had a perfect address position and took his club back into a perfect position at the top of the swing and smacked the ball, time after time. I felt he was like Mozart."

Duran's comparison was incredibly accurate. Wolfgang Amadeus Mozart is best known for his beautiful operas and other compositions that he wrote as an adult. But as a child, he performed on the harpsichord and other instruments for the royalty of Europe in the mid-eighteenth century. All serious music lovers of his time knew who he was.

Amazed that a four-year-old could control his club well enough to hit a ball high, low, or medium, Duran began teaching Tiger. Like Earl, he set Tiger pars for each hole based on Tiger's ability. Even though Tiger was only four, his par for the entire course was only thirteen shots higher than an adult's. By the time he was five, Tiger had beaten his par by eight shots. He had also graduated to a full set of clubs, specially sized for his small body. He continued to hone his game, playing with Duran, Earl, and anyone else who cared to be amazed.

"The best thing about those practices was that my father always kept it fun," Tiger recalled later. "Golf for me has always been a labor of love and pleasure."

In some ways, said Tiger's father, the discrimination at the navy course helped Tiger, because it led him to Heartwell, where he could work on his game. His years there provided basic training that would pay off big in the future. "Strange how unwelcome, unforeseen circumstances can shape our lives," Earl said.

> When Tiger was young, Earl focused on developing the boy's mental toughness. During a shot—when everyone is supposed to be quiet—Earl would make noise. He tried to jar Tiger's concentration. Tiger's sheer stubbornness helped him ignore these distractions.

Competitions

Baseball has T-ball and then Little League. Football has Pop Warner. In the golf world, junior competitions and tournaments are held across the country. The American Junior Golf Association sponsors a series of national events for golfers in similar age groups. The competition can be fierce.

Tiger joined the Southern California Junior Golf Association when he was just four years old. The lowest age bracket was ten and under, so at first, he played against much older kids. His first win came in his fourth match, against a ten-year-old.

Tiger sank his first hole-in-one on May 12, 1982, at the age of six.

Already, Tiger and his family were taking the sport very seriously. They made sacrifices for him to play and compete. The tournaments cost money to enter. They were sometimes held far away and at very early hours. "He never complained when the alarm went off," said Earl years later. "I can still remember cracking one eye at 4 A.M. . . . .

[Kultida] and Tiger were preparing to leave for a nine-hole tournament a 90-minute drive away."

Tiger did very well during the weekend and summer matches, though he did not always win. By the time he was in second grade, he had already played and won an international tournament against kids from all over the world. His skills grew as he practiced and competed.

As he grew, his aptitude for the sport became more and more obvious. Earl Woods promised Tiger he would

Junior success: At the age of five, Tiger was already winning trophies in the junior category. He poses with what his mom called his first "big" trophy.

For the crowd: Tiger displays his hitting abilities at a golf clinic. He was only six years old at the time.

have "as good a chance as any of those country club kids" to succeed at the sport. But lessons and tournaments and just plain playing added up to a considerable amount of money. Counting travel costs, the junior tournaments Tiger entered cost his family about twenty-five to thirty thousand dollars a year.

The Woodses weren't rich, and Tiger didn't make any money playing. They scrimped and saved and funded some of the travel with a loan. The family didn't take a nongolf holiday while Tiger was young. Earl and sometimes Kultida accompanied him to every competition on the road. Earl decided he would take early retirement from his job at McDonnell Douglas. That would give him the time

Focused: Tiger lines up a putt at the Junior World Championship in San Diego, California, in 1984. The eight-year-old went on to win the tournament and many more across the country.

he needed to go with Tiger to the top junior golfing events across the country.

Perspective

As important as golf was, it remained only part of Tiger's life as he neared junior high school. His parents insisted that he not take time from his studies to play. While he might choose not to play baseball so he could concentrate on golf, he had no choice when it came to school-work. Studies were first.

Besides golf, Tiger did things most other American kids did. He played Nintendo and Ping-Pong, rode his bike around the neighborhood, and spent time fooling around with buddies. He and his friends used to play tackle football in a parking lot near his home. He was a very good runner, and when he reached junior high, he joined the cross-country team for a season.

Tiger's mother practiced Buddhism, an ancient religion several hundred years older than Christianity. She passed on its beliefs to her son, emphasizing the need for humility and meditation as he grew. The religion proved a good balance to the worldly distractions that assaulted him.

A Personal Milestone

Tiger got better and better as he grew. Part of his improvement came because he was growing up physically. He didn't need anyone to cut down clubs for him or to let him use a tee on every shot. Another part of his improvement came from his study of the game and his unrelenting practice.

"I would be walking along, carrying his bag, and with those long legs of his, he was gone. He'd say, 'Hurry up, Dad.' I said, 'Are you at your ball yet? No. Are you ready for another club? No. When you are, I'll be there.'"

—Earl Woods, on carrying Tiger's bag in junior tournaments

As they grow, many boys measure themselves against their fathers. They strive to see if they are as good as their role models. When they are, they are often ready for an important rite of passage into adulthood. In Tiger's case, he had a ready-made means of measuring himself against his dad—golf.

Tiger kept getting better, knowing that someday he'd be able to beat his father. Earl was a good golfer himself. He was also very competitive. He wasn't about to give up easily. But he, too, knew that the day he lost to Tiger fair and square would eventually come.

The day came on November 28, 1987, about a month before Tiger's twelfth birthday. Father and son set out for the Long Beach navy course. Playing with some friends, Tiger and Earl were close through the first nine holes. Tiger birdied, or shot 1 under par, on the tough

Father and son: Tiger and Earl were competitive golfers, even with each other. Tiger finally beat his dad in a match played in 1987, at the age of eleven.

fourteenth hole to tie his dad. They stayed neck and neck for the next two holes. Then on number seventeen, Tiger managed to drop his ball with his second shot—another birdie. Earl took three shots to sink his ball. "Daddy," Tiger said, "I'm ahead of you."

The round ended with Tiger one shot ahead of his dad. Tiger still had a long way to go before he could compete with the best golfers in the world. His dad and mom still had to ferry him around and accompany him to tournaments. But he had met an important challenge at a young age. He had beaten the man who had first taught him the game. Tiger Woods was ready to step out on his own.

Island green: The water hazard surrounding the seventeenth green at Sawgrass attracts the balls of good and bad golfers alike. Tiger made a bold shot on this hole during the 1994 U.S. Amateur competition.

Breaking Out

Tiger Woods took a breath as he walked toward the tee at the Sawgrass golf course in Ponte Vedra Beach, Florida. The eighteen-year-old was playing in the last round of the 1994 U.S. Amateur Championship. Already it had been a tough match. In the third round, he had been matched against Buddy Alexander, the golf coach of the University of Florida Gators. The contest came down to the back nine, or last nine holes. The crowd had included a few racists, including one who said rather loudly to another, "Who do you think these people are rooting for, the nigger or the Gator coach?"

Tiger had hung in there and won the third round and the next. For the final, he was matched against a friend, Trip Kuehne. Kuehne, four years older, took an early lead in the long final match. Entering afternoon play, Tiger was down by four strokes.

He knew he could come back. As Tiger walked toward the tee to start the final eighteen holes, his dad took hold of him and pulled him aside. "Son," Earl said, "let the legend grow."

Tiger nodded and went to address (prepare to swing at) the ball. It was a great pep talk—simple and to the point. The only problem was, at first it didn't seem to work. Tiger fell five strokes back on the first six holes. But then Kuehne began to falter slightly. Tiger began to play daringly, taking do-or-die shots—and making them. Hole after hole, he fought back and tied the match at the end of the sixteenth hole.

The cup on the seventeenth green at Sawgrass lay very close to the edge of the water hazard. Most golfers attempted to place the ball on the broad side of the green, farther away from the water. This strategy usually cost them at least one stroke. Their logic was simple—hitting the ball from the tee so it would fall next to the hole and not in the water was almost impossible.

The seventeenth hole at Sawgrass is famous. The green is an island—a very small island. Every year about 120,000 golf balls end up in the water at the seventeenth. Some golfers pay the fee to play the entire course just to play number seventeen. A long-time PGA Tour caddie got his dying wish for his ashes to be spread over the water at the seventeenth.

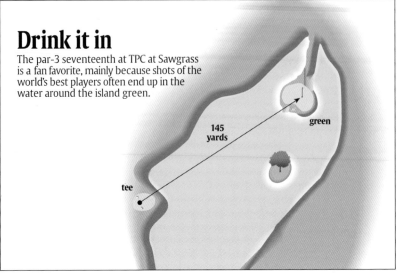

Drink it in

The par-3 seventeenth at TPC at Sawgrass is a fan favorite, mainly because shots of the world's best players often end up in the water around the island green.

145 yards

green

tee

Source: PGA Tour

By Dave Merrill, USA TODAY

Woods chose a pitching wedge and hit a soft fade into the wind. The golf ball shot high in the air. It seemed to hover there, trying to decide whether to land in the water or on the green. If it landed in the water, the match would essentially be over. Woods would have to take penalty shots and fall behind. If it landed on the green, Woods would be positioned to take a powerful lead.

The ball fell on the grass and bounced. Its roll took it within a foot and a half of the water—but it was still on the green. "Divine intervention," said Kuehne's father after the fantastic shot that clinched the championship for his son's friend.

Top Coaches

The victory at Sawgrass made Tiger the youngest person ever to win the U.S. Amateur. Though just eighteen, he already was a polished competitor with many trophies to display. Tiger won the U.S. Junior Amateur in 1991 at the age of fifteen and then again in 1992 to become the first golfer to win the event twice. A first-place finish in 1993 gave him an unprecedented three in a row. He was, by any measure, an excellent golfer.

Junior amateur: In 1991 Tiger holds the first of three trophies for winning the U.S. Junior Amateur Championship. He went on to win in 1992 and 1993.

This wasn't an accident. Tiger had taken his natural skills and honed them through practice and more practice. He had also received very good coaching. Besides Rudy Duran and his father, Tiger had advanced with the help of different coaches who worked on aspects of his game. John Anselmo, the head teaching pro at Meadowlark Golf Club in Huntington Beach, California, worked with him on his swing, after Duran left Southern California for another job. By working on Woods's mechanics, Anselmo helped the athlete add power without making his drives hook, or curve, in the air.

Tiger got even more help from one of the country's top swing coaches, Claude "Butch" Harmon. Harmon had taught one of Tiger's heroes, Greg Norman, as well as other golf superstars. In 1993 Harmon went to work refining Tiger's swing, helping him get more control and accuracy in his game.

"Tiger showed me some of the shots that he could hit, and I made some suggestions to him at the time that would make him more consistent," Harmon said. "It was nothing special but I guess he liked the results that he saw." Harmon often worked over the phone or after watching videotape of Tiger. Golf reporter Tim Rosaforte said that

Harmon could tell how Tiger's swing was going just by asking him the question, "Where's the ball starting?"

Harmon's ability to give Woods advice over the phone—and Tiger's ability to use it—was one of the factors that helped Woods win his first Amateur Championship. After a phone call during the tournament, Tiger immediately put his coach's advice to work.

Tiger's coaches weren't all working on his mechanics. Navy captain and clinical psychologist Jay Brunza, a golfer and friend of his father's, helped him with the psychological aspects of the game. Brunza also caddied and played with him occasionally. He taught Tiger techniques for focusing and keeping the mental edge that is so important in competition. Tiger also listened to tapes on relaxation techniques as well as pep talks that helped him stay poised and confident on the course.

As a young player, Tiger was often shorter and slighter than his competitors. He tells the story that he once found himself intimidated by another young golfer who was only a year older but who far outweighed him. The other player was also several inches taller. Earl's advice? To remember that golf requires skill, smarts, and courage—it's not a game of size or bulk. Tiger vowed not to be intimidated ever again.

A Rush of Success

By his teen years, Tiger had already settled on his course. He knew he wanted to be a golf professional. "I want to tear it up on the [PGA] Tour," he told a reporter when he was still competing as a junior. Tiger's grades were nearly perfect, and he also wanted to continue his schooling. He was already thinking about what he wanted to study in college.

Tiger reports that as a child on rainy days, he'd turn his parents' living room into a chipping area. Chips are short, high shots. For example, he'd aim a chip over the coffee table to land just short of the fireplace. His chips were so quiet his mom never knew what he was doing.

Tiger's high school years had rushed by in a blur. He spent an enormous amount of time playing golf—summers, vacations, weekends, and hours and hours after school. But he also studied hard and found time for fun things. He loved *The Simpsons,* a popular animated TV show, and he videotaped pro wrestling matches. He also developed a love of McDonald's and other fast-food restaurants.

Seeing only golf: In the summer of 1993, Tiger took part in the Junior World Championship, which he'd won five times before at different age levels of play.

As a freshman, Tiger made the varsity golf team at Western High School in Anaheim. With his first U.S. Junior Amateur win, his teammates and coach quickly saw that he was something special. Adding on two more championship wins set him apart. In 1993 Tiger took home the coveted Dial Award, given annually to the best high school male and female athletes in the country. But many, many golfers rocket to success

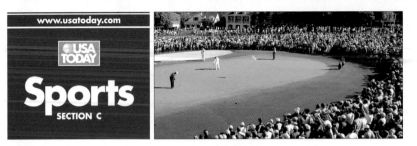

February 25, 1993

Woods shows pros he's a quick study

<u>From the Pages of</u>
<u>USA TODAY</u>

PACIFIC PALISADES, CA -- A year ago, playing in the Nissan Los Angeles Open was overwhelming for high school sophomore Eldrick Woods.

This week, "Tiger" Woods, 17, returns, acting as if this is just one of several guest appearances on the PGA Tour.

A lot has happened to Woods in the last year. The first to win two U.S. Junior championships, he has traveled more than his entire high school class combined, playing tournaments all across the USA.

"In some ways, playing junior tournaments is tougher than the PGA Tour," Woods said. "Some of our tournaments are Friday through Sunday, others are Tuesday through Friday, then maybe Sunday through Wednesday. I could be gone four or five weeks and play five or six events."

Woods says his father, Earl, a former Army lieutenant colonel, is the boss as far as scheduling.

Woods has a 4.3 grade-point average on a 4.0 scale because he's taking accelerated courses.

"I have to decide whether to pick a school that emphasizes golf or academics," he said. "I'll make some trips, then sign this fall."

—Steve Hershey, February 25, 1993

as juniors, only to flame out as they advance to college and the higher levels of play. Tiger still had to prove himself in the long run.

Coming Home

As he wrapped up his high school years, Tiger was in an enviable position. College coaches came to him, trying to recruit him. They offered scholarships and promised him the chance to play the sport at a very high level, with excellent coaches and well-groomed golf courses.

Tiger narrowed down his college search to two places—the University of Nevada at Las Vegas (UNLV) and Stanford University in California. Both colleges have excellent sports programs. He visited UNLV and was impressed by the golf coach as well as the excellent facilities the golf teams used.

But then he went to Stanford. Stanford's golf coach, Wally Goodwin, had been corresponding with Tiger for several years, ever since he saw a small feature on him in *Sports Illustrated.* Goodwin, like many others, had taken notice of Tiger's junior victories and realized his great potential. Many top athletes had Stanford diplomas on their walls. The college had a beautiful campus and some of the best teachers in the country. It also promoted academic excellence. Its students included some of the brightest people in the world. "I knew I was home," Tiger told his parents when he returned from his visit.

Terrible Dancer, Great Golfer

As a freshman on the Stanford golf team, Tiger was treated more or less like any freshman. He accepted the "rollaway," the cot used when three teammates shared a two-bedroom hotel room. He had to put up with a dumb nickname imposed by the seniors. He became one of the guys, although an immensely talented one.

Tiger joined the fraternity Sigma Chi and there allegedly earned the nickname Dynamite for his dancing. His friends didn't intend the name to be a compliment. "It was terrible," recalled a fellow student named Jake Poe. "On the dance floor, it looked like he was blowing up a house, or pumping up a bike," added another friend and golf teammate, Eric Crum.

But if he wasn't very adept at dancing, Woods was great at golf and getting even better. In his first collegiate competition, he shot a 4-under-par 68 to win the Tucker Invitational at the University of New Mexico in Albuquerque.

Tiger is among many Sigma Chi members around the country. Fellow golfers Notah Begay and Luke Donald were also part of the fraternity. Football coaches Mike Holmgren and Mike Ditka were members. Celebrities Brad Pitt, David Hartman, and John Wayne belonged too.

Tiger had always stood out not simply because of his golf but because of his studies. At Stanford he studied economics and met many academic achievers. A fellow freshman had already taken every math course the college offered. He was tearing up math books the way Tiger tore up golf courses, something Tiger admired. Woods became an avid reader, devouring books during his off time instead of watching TV. And he found time to go to at least some of the parties that college students enjoy.

Target and Symbol

College was not all fun, however. Once, while returning to his dorm, Woods was robbed at knifepoint. The robber smashed his jaw and took his watch and a gold chain. Fortunately, Tiger was not seriously injured. And the robber missed his wallet and something more valuable than money—a four hundred-year-old miniature Buddha that usually hung from the chain. Tiger wasn't wearing the family heirloom that night.

The robber called Tiger by his name, even though Woods didn't know him. Fame had shown its dark side to the young man. He was easy to single out because he was so well known. The color of his skin also made Tiger easy to single out. Many people treated him as if he represented all African Americans. As a symbol, Tiger was sometimes criticized, by blacks as well as whites.

In October 1994, Stanford's golf team traveled to the Jerry Pate Invitational at Shoal Creek in Birmingham, Alabama. Four years

Team picture: Tiger Woods *(back row, fourth from left)* stands with his team-mates for a team picture in 1994. Notah Begay stands to Tiger's left, and Jerry Chang is in the front row, third from left. Both players have remained Tiger's lifelong friends.

earlier, the club's founder had openly admitted that African Americans weren't allowed as members. Even though an African American person was later given an honorary membership, many people thought the gesture was just for show. A great deal of prejudice was still at the club and in the local community.

Tiger and his teammates played the first two rounds. They did fairly well, with Tiger trailing the leader by three strokes with one more day of play to go. But then controversy erupted. Several African Americans told Coach Goodwin that Tiger shouldn't be playing at Shoal Creek. Instead, they suggested that Tiger and the rest of the team should boycott it because of its racial prejudice. And, they added, if he didn't, they would protest.

"My first concern was the safety of my team," said Goodwin later. "But we weren't about to turn around and fly back to California and not fulfill our obligation. On the very same team are a full-blooded Navajo

Indian [Notah Begay] and a Japanese-American [William Yanagisawa] and a Chinese-American [Jerry Chang], and here they're picking on Tiger. It was ludicrous."

The weather helped the golfers dodge the protesters. Hard rain gave the organizers an easy excuse to say the course was underwater and closed to the public. The protesters stayed outside the front gate. Tiger shot a 5 under par and came from behind to win.

The Big Time

Tiger's victory in the 1994 U.S. Amateur tournament gave him an automatic invitation to try out for the big time: the 1995 Masters Tournament at Augusta, Georgia. Though he had played in several professional events already, the Masters was far and away the most important event he had ever entered. Pros and amateurs alike regard the Masters, with its long history, as one of the sport's special competitions. Only the very best golfers in the world can walk on Augusta's fairways and greens at tournament time.

During his first time at Augusta National golf club as an amateur, Tiger got lost and accidentally stumbled into the locker room set aside for people who have won the Masters. He told himself, "I'm gonna have my name in here, one day I will have it in here." And two years later, he did.

By this time, the media had carried many stories on Woods's potential and the fact that he was a young black man in a sport usually played by older white males. The press covered Tiger as if he were already a star when he came to Augusta. He attracted a large crowd when he teed off on opening day. His first shot was a beauty—a drive of 280 yards, easily clearing a difficult sand trap. He continued to play well, posting an even-par 72, which tied him for thirty-fourth in the field. He shot 72 in the next round as well, finishing high enough to stay in contention for the final rounds.

But in the third round, Tiger played poorly, posting a 5-over-par 77. That left him far off the pace. Even so, he managed a 72 on the last day of play, coming back with birdies on three of the last four holes. The showing was more than respectable, considering that Tiger was still very young.

He didn't think he had lived up to his full potential. Others agreed. Some observers seemed to relish the fact that Tiger hadn't placed with the leaders. Members of the media criticized him for not giving interviews at times and felt that his father arranged some of his actions. Earl, who could be loud and outspoken with criticism as well as praise, was called a stage father who pushed and controlled his son. Through it all, Tiger struggled to keep his focus.

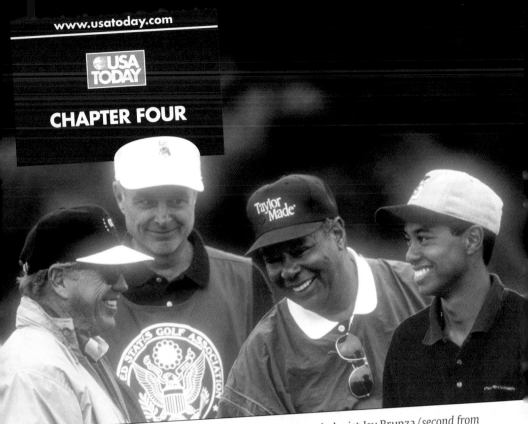

Team Tiger: Coach Butch Harmon (*left*) and sports psychologist Jay Brunza (*second from left*) celebrate Tiger's 1995 U.S. Amateur Championship win.

Becoming a Professional

After the 1995 Masters, Tiger Woods went back to Stanford, where he had other things to think about—like a major exam in history. Though he still valued academics, he was beginning to think that his schoolwork was keeping him from reaching his full potential as a golfer.

At the same time, the different rules governing amateur and collegiate sports chafed the budding superstar. In early October 1995, Tiger went to dinner with one of golf's all-time greats, Arnold Palmer. Palmer, who is rich as well as famous, paid for dinner. When the National Collegiate Athletic Association (NCAA), the governing board of college athletics, found out, it decided that the free meal violated rules against college athletes receiving special benefits. Stanford suspended Tiger from competition.

"I don't need this," Tiger told his parents angrily when he gave them the news. The suspension lasted only a day, but his parents saw the NCAA dispute as the beginning of the end of Woods's college career.

Tiger stayed on for the rest of the school year. He won a second Amateur Championship in 1995 and easily dom-

Liftoff: Tiger lifts his father off the ground in jubilation after winning the 1995 championship, his second amateur championship in a row.

inated on the college level during his sophomore year. Even with a heavy course load, Tiger took seven first-place finishes. He won the NCAA Championships at the end of May 1996 and the Jack Nicklaus

College Player of the Year award the next month. By then, sponsors on the professional tour were clamoring for him to compete in their events, as an amateur or not. The question wasn't whether he should turn professional, but when.

Endorsement Money

Turning pro would mean that Tiger could accept prize money when he won. Golfers earn big monetary prizes for winning or placing high in a PGA Tour event. Top prizes can be more than half a million dollars.

IN F🔍CUS

Amateur versus Professional

In one way, the difference between amateurs and professionals is simple. Amateurs can't play for money, but professionals can. In most sports, playing for money increases the pressure of competition. A pro athlete must agree to play in a certain number of events. He or she must also follow the rules set forth by the league or governing body of the sport.

In the United States, the PGA Tour organizes men's professional golf events throughout the year. It also helps arrange TV coverage. Two other organizations are also involved in the sport. The United States Golf Association (USGA) sets golf rules and promotes the sport in various ways. The USGA sponsors the U.S. Open every year. The PGA of America is an association for teaching golf professionals. It runs the PGA Championship.

Not just anyone can compete on the PGA Tour. While there are different ways to enter individual contests, to compete on the year-long tour, golfers must demonstrate that they are among the best in the sport. That means they have to do well in a number of events. Only the top 125 golfers—measured by their prize money in PGA-Tour-sanctioned events—receive player's cards, making them full-fledged members of the PGA Tour.

Other players with good scores can earn thousands. Over the course of a year's play, many competitors can take home millions.

Other payoffs happen as well. Like other athletes, famous golfers are paid to give speeches and appear at certain events, like golf exhibitions and souvenir signings. Many tournaments outside the United States offer first-class golfers appearance fees, which are forbidden in the PGA Tour. Top golfers can make $100,000 or $250,000 by agreeing to compete overseas. Someone very famous can make even more.

And then there are product endorsements. Many companies want to use famous people to help sell their products. The companies reach agreements with stars. Sometimes, stars simply agree to use a company's equipment or other products. The firms hope fans see that their sports hero uses a certain type of glove, for example, and will look for that glove in the store. In other cases, companies hire stars to make commercials and act as representatives. They attempt to tie their product to the star's image.

To help arrange such deals, most pro athletes hire an agent. The agent represents the athlete in business matters. By the summer of 1996, Tiger and his family had settled on the International Management Group (IMG) as his representative. Tiger and his family had met an IMG representative some years before. Earl had also worked for IMG as a scout, so it wasn't surprising that Tiger chose that company.

Even before being officially hired, IMG had lined up potential endorsement deals for Tiger. The biggest was a five-year, $40 million agreement with Nike. It was an incredible contract for an athlete who had yet to win a professional event.

Swoosh

Nike manufactures athletic equipment, shoes, and clothes. Once Tiger turned pro, the cap and shirt he wore at golf matches always had the Nike trademark, a "swoosh," on them. He also began making commercials and advertisements for Nike.

"What Michael Jordan did for basketball, [Woods] absolutely can do for golf," said the head of Nike, Phil Knight. "The world has not seen anything like what he's going to do for the sport. It's almost art. I wasn't alive to see Monet paint, but I am alive to see Tiger play golf, and that's pretty great."

Michael Jordan is one of the greatest basketball players of all time. His endorsements had helped Nike become one of the most successful athletic equipment companies. While Jordan continued to serve as the company's spokesperson, in some ways, Nike had found his successor in Tiger.

Nike wanted to capitalize on Tiger's fame. But he would benefit as well. Not only did he get a large sum of money, but the commercials would also give him a great deal of exposure. The fact that a successful sports company had chosen to make him such an important spokesperson would also help his image. That would make his endorsement even more valuable in the future.

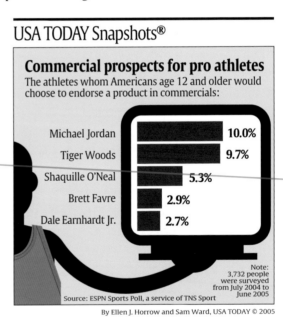

USA TODAY Snapshots®

Commercial prospects for pro athletes
The athletes whom Americans age 12 and older would choose to endorse a product in commercials:

Michael Jordan	**10.0%**
Tiger Woods	**9.7%**
Shaquille O'Neal	**5.3%**
Brett Favre	**2.9%**
Dale Earnhardt Jr.	**2.7%**

Note: 3,732 people were surveyed from July 2004 to June 2005

Source: ESPN Sports Poll, a service of TNS Sport

By Ellen J. Horrow and Sam Ward, USA TODAY © 2005

Endorsement deals have been around for a long time, but it was unusual for someone who had yet to compete as a pro to receive such a big contract. Nike was taking a risk, since something might happen to Tiger to make him look like a bad spokesperson. He might not be able to stand the pressure of turning pro and might lose a lot of events, for example.

But several reasons made the deal a good move. Tiger already played well. He was already known beyond golf. And besides being a great athlete, he was a mostly soft-spoken, clean-living young man. No dark clouds lurked in his past, and none were likely in his future. He didn't use drugs and didn't fool around with women. Advertisers didn't have to worry that he would be involved in a scandal that might hurt their sales.

Even more important, the media had already begun to spin a simple, positive story line about him. He was a young African American man trying to integrate the top ranks of golf. Nike would use that image and even help shape it in ads.

Woods wasn't the first African American golfer. He always made that clear. He also emphasized that he was Asian as well as African American, Native American, and Caucasian. Still, most people saw him as African American. And most people, including golfers, associated the sport with whites. Many people—whites as well as blacks—would root for Tiger to succeed because his victories symbolized racial justice to them.

His youth also helped him. The popular image of golf was as a sport for older men. The fact that someone barely out of his teens could compete and win made that person unique in the public's eye. Any company wishing to portray itself as youthful could do so simply by using him as a spokesperson.

"Are You Ready?"

None of the big money deals could happen until Tiger turned pro. As the summer of 1996 wound down, he prepared for the U.S. Amateur, the championship he had won twice before. As if to prove that it was time to make his move, he won for a third straight time—something no one had ever done. "It's time to go," he told his parents when he got back from the tournament.

A few days later in Milwaukee, Wisconsin, Tiger Woods confirmed that he planned to turn pro. He quit school, although he said he hoped

Make it three: Tiger is all smiles as he hoists the U.S. Amateur Championship trophy for the third time in 1996.

to return to his studies someday. The endorsement money immediately poured in. Nike finalized its contract for five years and a total of $40 million, with a $7.5 million signing bonus. Titleist, a major manufacturer of golf balls, golf clubs, and other golfing equipment, offered him $3 million a year. That contract was soon negotiated into a five-year deal that paid him $20 million and called for him to use Titleist clubs as soon as the company could design a set for him. By the end of 1996, his endorsement fees were dwarfed only by basketball star Michael Jordan's earnings.

With endorsement money, Tiger and Earl Woods founded the Tiger Woods Foundation. Its goal is to inspire children, especially those from lower-income families, to achieve their dreams. The foundation offers scholarships, gives grants to communities, and sets up junior golf teams and clinics.

www.usatoday.com

USA TODAY

Sports

SECTION C

August 29, 1996

Woods enjoys pro life, still pinches pennies

From the Pages of
USA TODAY

MILWAUKEE, WI -- Just call him a paper Tiger. Although Tiger Woods has agreed to more than $40 million in endorsement contracts, he's still a multimillionaire on paper only.

``I haven't seen any checks in the mail yet,'' Woods said Wednesday, laughing at himself. ``I'm still broke. I guess I'll still be eating at McDonald's for a while longer.''

Woods, who won his third consecutive U.S. Amateur title Sunday, turned pro Tuesday. He plays for money for the first time today in the PGA Tour Greater Milwaukee Open, beginning his round at 2:36 p.m. ET.

Wednesday, in his first news conference as a pro, Woods' youthful exuberance showed.

How is he adjusting to life as a pro?

``It's great,'' Woods said. ``I even got a courtesy car. I'm not old enough to rent a car, but I still got one.''

But he's still accustomed to the frugal life he lived for two years as a Stanford student. ``When we went to dinner (Tuesday), everyone said I was a pro now and they expected me to pick up the tab, so I pulled out some $25 (restaurant) gift certificates I had,'' Woods laughed.

Don't expect frugality from Titleist/Footjoy Worldwide, which is paying Woods $3 million over the next three years to endorse equipment.

``Titleist worldwide will do in excess of $500 million this year,'' CEO Wally Uihlein said. ``I'm looking to get away from the pack, and that's what Tiger represents. It reinforces that Titleist is not just another golf brand.''

Some of Woods' humor rubbed off on his father, Earl, who worried when negotiations with Titleist and Nike accelerated when Tiger decided to turn pro. ``It's what you call last-minute Christmas shopping with no money.''

—Jerry Bonkowski, August 29, 1996

Nike used Tiger's image in ads and commercials right away. One of the first prominent ads declared, "I shot in the 70s when I was 8. I shot in the 60s when I was 12. I won the U.S. Junior Amateur when I was 14. . . . I won the U.S. Amateur when I was 18. I played in the Masters when I was 19. I am the only man to win three consecutive U.S. Amateur titles. There are still golf courses in the United States that I cannot play because of the color of my skin. I'm told I'm not ready for you. Are you ready for me?"

People immediately objected to the line about discrimination, saying that it was incorrect. Tiger Woods could play anywhere he wanted. He was so famous that people would love to have him at their course.

Jim Thorpe, another African American on the PGA Tour, pointed out that earlier African American golfers had faced real prejudice. "Every time Charlie Sifford won a tournament, they changed the rule at the Masters so he couldn't play," said Thorpe, who criticized Nike, not Tiger. "With Lee Elder and Charlie, you'd hear the N-word, but I didn't have to go through it," Thorpe added.

Nike responded that the line was meant symbolically—that some African Americans were still not allowed to play at courses or join clubs in the United States. The tone of the ad was aggressive and combative. While Tiger Woods is a fierce competitor on the golf course, in person he is a soft-spoken gentleman. Golf has a more gentlemanly image than many other sports, such as football or basketball. The Nike ads rubbed many in the sport the wrong way.

"We knew that Tiger turned on the thousand-watt smile whenever a TV camera was around but could be short and surly with those he didn't deem important," said John Feinstein, a sportswriter. Feinstein soon became well known for his attempts to debunk what he called "the Tiger myth." The Nike ads soon changed. And, like Michael Jordan before him, Tiger Woods became an athlete so famous he could be referred to and recognized by a single name: Tiger.

That smile: Tiger shows off his winning smile and appealing personality while taking questions at a news conference in 1996.

Moving Up, Then Down

Despite the big contracts, major advertising campaigns, and media attention, Tiger Woods still needed to prove himself. Perhaps tired by all the hoopla, he finished well down in the standings at his first pro event, in Milwaukee. Over the next few weeks, he began a slow but steady march toward higher finishes. He took fifth in the Quad City Classic and then third in the B.C. Open. After that, he needed only a few decent showings to earn his tour card.

But the stress of his new life got to him when he arrived in Pine Mountain, Georgia, for the Buick Challenge. After a practice round, he decided he was too tired to compete. He canceled and went home, missing not just the tournament but also an important awards dinner scheduled in his honor. As the top college golfer in the country the year before, he had won the Fred Haskins Award. The award would have been presented at a dinner at Pine Mountain. The dinner was canceled, and critics besieged him.

Some later pointed out that it was the first professional event Tiger had been to without his dad or his coach, Butch Harmon. But Tiger didn't use that as an excuse, admitting a few days later that he had been immature to blow off the dinner. "I am human," he said in a *Golf World* column, "and I do make mistakes." His father said Tiger would make good on the money the sponsors had paid for the occasion. It was a low point in Tiger's early career.

A First First

Two weeks later, Tiger traveled to the Las Vegas Invitational. He was no longer tired. As the tournament went on, his focus sharpened. He shot a 64 on the last round, ending tied with Davis Love III. The two men began a playoff on the eighteenth hole.

"Great playing, Tiger," said Love as they got ready to shoot it out. "Thanks, stud," said Tiger, outwardly very loose and

Rookie win: Tiger raises the trophy for winning the Las Vegas Invitational. He beat Davis Love III in a one-hole shoot-out to capture his first PGA Tour victory.

cool. Love walloped a good tee shot to begin. Woods took his 3-wood from the bag and followed with a good shot a short distance behind Love's. That gave Tiger the first shot, often a psychological advantage in a shoot-out. Tiger put his ball only eighteen feet from the cup.

Feeling the pressure, Love swung his 7-iron too quickly. The ball landed in a bunker just beyond the hole. Love hung tough. His shot out of the trap landed on the green, six feet from the flag. All Tiger had to do to win was hit the middle-range putt. But it was a bit too far for him. His ball stopped two feet from the cup. He tapped it in, still confident. The best Love could do was sink his six-footer and be tied. They would go on to another hole. Love addressed the ball well, but it slid below the cup. Tiger Woods had won his first PGA Tour tournament. Everyone knew it wouldn't be his last.

Passing it on: In addition to learning how to compete from his parents, Tiger also learned how to give back. *Above:* He helps a young golfer perfect his swing during a golf clinic run by the Tiger Woods Foundation.

What's in the Bag?

Golfers use different types of clubs, depending on where they are on a golf course. Clubs can be divided into three general categories: woods, irons, and specialty clubs like the putter.

The most numerous clubs are woods and irons. Each group has several sizes, from large to small. They are numbered according to size and shape. In both cases, the lower the number, the farther the club is expected to send a ball when hit. However, there is a trade-off. For most golfers, the lower-numbered clubs give less loft, or height, on a shot and less accuracy.

Woods are often thought of as the long-distance clubs. They can send a ball far down a fairway. They are called woods because the head (the part of the club that hits the ball) was originally made of wood. While the heads are no longer always made of wood, the clubs' general shape and purpose remains the same. They have large, round heads with a flat surface for striking the ball. The shaft, which connects the head to the handle, is very long.

Wood sizes begin at 1 and extend to 5. The 1-wood is called a driver. The driver and the 3-wood are the most common clubs for teeing off because they can hit the ball a great distance. An average recreational male golfer would be expected to hit a ball at least two hundred yards when teeing off. Tiger Woods averages about three hundred yards in competition.

Golfers need more control and loft for shorter shots on the fairway or in the rough. There, golfers generally use an iron. The heads of irons are made of metal. They have shorter shafts, and their heads are more angled than woods. Like woods, the higher the number of the club, the higher a ball will go. But it won't travel as far.

driver

iron

sand wedge

Irons with low numbers—1 through 4—are called long irons because they are best used for long shots. On the other end of the spectrum are the short irons, 8 and 9, along with the pitching wedge.

The two groups of golf clubs overlap. Some golfers prefer to use a long iron instead of a wood in certain situations, and vice versa. Selecting the proper club is one of the great arts of the game. In some situations, the right club is obvious. A special club, called a sand wedge, is used when a ball lands in a bunker or sand trap. This club is sharply angled to help lift the ball from the trap.

On the green, a putter is used. The head of this club is small and very flat. Putters allow golfers to control the direction of the ball with great precision.

The rules of golf limit golfers to carrying just fourteen clubs. The rules also govern the shape and construction of the clubs.

putter

First Masters win: Fans have come to love the exuberance of Tiger's fist pump. But it was especially meaningful at the 1997 Masters, which he won for the first time while setting a course record of 12 under par.

Promise Fulfilled

They came past the magnificent magnolia trees, up the lane to the clubhouse, down the long, expansive fairways. They stood patiently, along exquisite greens that shone like emeralds in the spring sun. They came in tens, hundreds, and thousands, sensing something special was about to happen this warm April day in Augusta, Georgia. With golf fans the world over, they sensed that on this day, April 13, 1997, the long-promised potential of Eldrick "Tiger" Woods was about to be fulfilled.

Tiger stepped out toward the tee. Two years earlier, he had become only the fourth African American in history to play at Augusta. This time, he was leading the Masters by nine strokes, an awesome edge with only one day left to play. But golf, especially at the Masters, can be a cruel heartbreaker. With so much prestige riding on a win here—with so many people looking on and with reporters everywhere—many men have crumbled on the last day.

Tiger certainly would have felt the strain if he had stopped to think about it. He'd known many triumphs, but he had also tasted failure. In the two years since playing his first Masters, Woods had undergone arthroscopic knee surgery, strained his rotator cuff, and even had a bout with food poisoning. He had won two PGA Tour events already that year, but he longed to wear the green jacket traditionally given to the Masters' winner. He longed to stand in the long line of champions.

Each year's Masters champion gets one green jacket to wear in public appearances. It must be returned to the club after one year.

The world could easily have crashed on Tiger's shoulders or at least messed up his tee shot. But Tiger Woods, just twenty-one, was so focused on his game and on where he wanted to put the ball that he couldn't feel pressure. He couldn't feel anything, except the exquisite smack of his club against the ball.

As the crowds cheered, Tiger made Augusta his. Every element of his game—the drives from the tee, the iron shots to the green and his putting—was perfect. By the time he raised his fist in triumph on the final hole, he had shot an incredible 18 under par for the tournament, setting a scoring record with a twelve-stroke lead.

He hugged his caddie, Mike "Fluff" Cowan. Then, holding his hat above his head, he walked to the edge of the green and found the

Sports
SECTION C

May 8, 1997

Giving Tiger Woods direction,
Earl Woods furnishes son love, lessons

From the Pages of
USA TODAY

ATLANTA, GA — It has come to be known as The Hug. It will forever remain etched in our minds as one of the most vivid memories in the history of The Masters and one of the most revealing moments in the relationship between a father and son.

After Tiger Woods, 21, sank his final putt at Augusta National last month to become the youngest to win The Masters—and the first of African-American and Asian heritage to win a major—he walked off the 18th green and headed straight for the burly, outstretched arms of his father Earl.

The two held onto each other tightly for several minutes, dissolving into tears of joy and relief.

President Clinton called The Hug "the best shot of the day," and evidently most of the 15 million TV viewers feel the same way.

"Not a day goes by when somebody doesn't mention it," says Earl, 65, in the midst of a two-week tour to promote his book, *Training a Tiger: A Father's Guide*

large arms of his speechless dad. Their hug celebrated the culmination of a quest that began more than twenty years before in a small suburban garage.

An Elder Statesman

Ceremonies and celebrations followed as 1996 winner Nick Faldo helped Tiger into the green jacket. Then he strode toward the putting *for Raising a Winner in Golf and Life*. "I've uniformly been told, 'I cried and cried when I saw you hug.' Men, women, parents, businessmen, athletes—people stop me in the streets.

"People can see honesty and honest emotions. If we're honest about our emotions, people will tune into them. Just like they gravitate toward happy people. I think that for most people who saw the hug, they realized how much they'd love to be there themselves."

The Hug has been a ritual for the pair since Tiger was 15

The hug: As mother, Kultida, watches, Earl and Tiger hug after his 1997 Masters win.

and won the first of three consecutive U.S. Golf Association junior titles. A hug is Earl's way of bringing closure to tournaments for Tiger. They provide a warm, safe place for the driven, single-minded prodigy to release his emotions and, most important, to always remind Tiger that, win or lose, he is loved.

Will there come a day when Tiger is too old for The Hug?

"Not unless I'm too old to be a parent," Earl says. "When you have a child, they're your child for life."

—Jill Lieber, May 8, 1997

green for another presentation. As he walked, he spotted a familiar face. "Lee, come here," he called to Lee Elder.

He embraced Elder, who in 1975 had become the first African American to play in the Masters. "Thanks for making this possible," Tiger told the older golfer. A tear appeared in Elder's eye.

"Augusta National had been a symbol of the old south, a place that clung to segregation," said John Feinstein, the golf writer and

Thanks to Lee: Wearing the green jacket worn by all Masters champions, Tiger warmly greets golfer Lee Elder, the first African American to play in the tournament.

a historian of the Masters. Even after Elder broke the color barrier, some resentment and prejudice remained. Tiger's victory confirmed his own greatness as a golfer. It also symbolized for many African Americans that they could succeed when allowed to compete on an equal basis.

Tiger didn't break the color line. As he told Elder, an earlier generation of African American golfers had paved the way for him and others. Tiger did face considerable prejudice, however. He received many hateful letters and was the subject of racist remarks by others on the tour. But his victory at the Masters answered the bigots. As Elder put it: "After today...no one will even turn their head to notice when a black person walks to the first tee."

Why So Good?

Tiger Woods would never have achieved his fame or his fortune without being skillful enough to win the Masters and many other PGA Tour events. There are several aspects to his greatness, beginning with his body and conditioning. Jack Nicklaus, whom many rank as the best golfer ever, says that the speed of Tiger's upper body as it winds against his lower body is critical on these shots.

"A friend of mine who owns professional videotape editing equipment that measures motion in thousandths of seconds compared the speed of Tiger's hips unwinding from the completion of the backswing to impact with a dozen or so other top Tour players. Tiger was 20 percent faster than anyone else, and as much as 50 percent quicker than some players," said Nicklaus.

Beyond his natural assets, Tiger's mechanics are extremely good. This is largely the result of training and practice. "He has beautiful basic fundamentals," Butch Harmon once said. "He has a perfect setup, perfect posture, a perfect grip. Everything about the way he sets up for a ball is very, very good. He's always had that his whole life. That's a credit to his dad and the other people he worked with."

The renowned golf coach offered one pointer for anyone watching Tiger drive: Watch his left foot. If it remains planted and balanced, the shot is likely to be a good one. Of course, Tiger himself often shows what he thinks of the shot with his reactions, jerking his hand up in triumph.

Even though he mostly has his temper under control, Tiger admits that he can still get mad at himself for a bad shot. His outbursts sometimes offend people, for which he says, "I wish I could vent without looking like a jerk. Unfortunately, I'm still working on it."

IN FOCUS

Watching Tiger

Harmon summed up Tiger's technique with four different points:

- Tiger has a very deliberate takeaway (the beginning of his golf swing).
- Tiger uses a quick, extreme turn of his shoulders that gives him a lot of power. This translates into distance on his drives.
- His long, athletic body is very flexible as well as strong. This helps him angle his shots properly. For Harmon one of the key flex points is Tiger's right knee, which twists elegantly on his best shots.
- Tiger uncoils his lower body very quickly, again giving him power and control.

Tiger stretch: Tiger carefully controls his whole body to hit his tee shots.

Beyond his physical assets, many fellow golfers cite his mental attitude. He manages a course well, choosing the right club for the situation. He is also extremely confident and mentally tough, able to overcome distractions. Just as important, Tiger has managed to remain motivated to get better while playing at a high level.

"Like all great champions, Tiger has the ability to raise his game when he has to," said Jay Brunza. "He's not going to burn out because he plays for his own joy and passion."

Pro golfer Jay Haas had a different insight after playing a tournament round with Tiger when the star did poorly. "What struck me about Tiger that day was, as angry as he was walking to the eighth tee, he didn't blow up and he didn't give up," Haas said. "The mark of a champion isn't how you play when everything is going right. It's how you play when you're struggling. He showed me something that day."

"As a golfer, he has tremendous ability, and the great thing is, he is still learning," the late Byron Nelson once said. "As well as he's been playing, he realizes to himself that he can play better. It's a trait all the great champions have."

Golf legend: Byron Nelson chats with Tiger after he won the Byron Nelson Classic in 1997. The tournament has been associated with Nelson since 1968. His record of eleven consecutive PGA Tour wins in 1945 still stands.

Tailing Off

Soon after Tiger's victory at the Masters, Earl went into the hospital for surgery. Tiger worried about his father. "There are more important things in life than golf," he said while Earl was in the hospital, cutting short a news conference. "I love my dad to death, and I'm going to see him right now."

Earl recovered, but Tiger and his family then faced a sad surprise. They discovered that the man Tiger had been named after, Vuong Dang Phong, had died many years before. The Vietnam War had ended, with Communist North Vietnam taking over South Vietnam. Tiger One, as Earl and Tiger called Colonel Phong, had been captured by the victors and had been put in a prison because he had fought against them. An enterprising reporter named Tom Callahan tracked down Phong's family in Vietnam and the United States, only to discover that Colonel Phong had been dead for more than twenty years.

Remembering Tiger One: With Colonel Vuong Dang Phong's son, Vuong Dang Phouc, looking on, Tiger and Earl review pictures of the man they called Tiger One in 1997.

"The effect of finding out about his death was stronger than I can explain," said Tiger. "From all I've heard, the three of us are alike. I'm more hot-tempered than my father is now. But he used to be like me—and so was Tiger One."

As Tiger matured, his ties to his father and mother remained strong. Tiger and his dad sometimes had heated arguments, especially when Earl thought Tiger hadn't played up to his potential. But they remained close. Earl and Kultida, however, began living separately even though they remained married. Earl said that they still loved each other, and they were often seen together at Tiger's tournaments.

Tiger won the Byron Nelson Classic and the Motorola Western Open after taking the Masters. Overall, 1997 was a fantastic year, propelling him to a number one ranking in the sport by mid-June. At twenty-one, he was the youngest golfer ever to grab that honor.

Tiger also shot to number one on the Official World Golf Ranking faster than anyone else ever has. After only forty-two weeks as a professional, on June 15, 1997, he became the number one golfer.

But he also had a few disappointing shows as the year went on. Though he didn't realize it, he was starting a slump that would carry into 1998. His second full year as a pro would frustrate and disappoint him and his fans.

Frustration: Tiger shows his disappointment with his play at a 1998 tournament in San Francisco, California.

Tiger Slam

Tiger stood over the ball, his long, lanky frame set like a pendulum. He was at the edge of the green. The hole lay a good distance away. He needed to sink the putt to start gaining ground on the leaders. His ankle was sore, and he was tired. But somehow he relaxed, his mind moving into a familiar, comfortable zone. As his weight shifted ever so slightly, his arms swung gently, like well-oiled parts in the works of a clock. His putter smacked the ball. It rolled along the green, riding a gentle lip on the surface. Then it slid down toward the cup, sliding and sliding, as if pulled by a magnet.

Except that it missed—not by much but enough for one more frustration in a tournament of frustrations. The 1997 Bell Canadian Open had turned into a disaster—for the first time since he had turned pro, Tiger failed to make the cut in a PGA Tour event.

Tiger rebounded to finish in the top three at three PGA Tour events in early 1998: the Mercedes-Benz Championship, the Buick Invitational, and the Nissan Open. But as the year went on, Tiger experienced a phenomenon common to all athletes—he was less than perfect. He failed to win a PGA Tour event all year.

No one has a perfect day every day. Still, fans and sports commentators expected Tiger to be, if not perfect, at least very, very good. When he wasn't, journalists said he was in a slump. Some statistics backed them up. Tiger started 1998 as the 60th best player on the tour. By the end of the year, he had dropped to 147th. Meanwhile, his driving and putting skills worsened. His balls regularly went off the fairway, and he often missed the hole with his putter.

But statistics don't tell the whole story. Tiger was still outplaying most of the pros on the PGA Tour. In fact, he believed he got better in 1998. "I think my ball flight's improved," Tiger said. "I'm

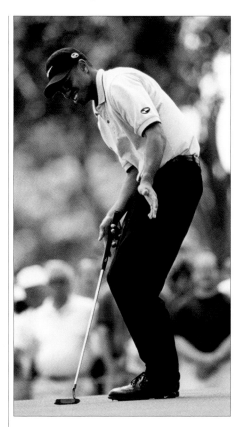

Poor putts: Only Tiger's mental toughness got him through an extended period of poor putting and driving in 1998.

able to play in conditions I've never been able to play before." Only when measured by his very extreme level of excellence could 1998 be considered a slump for Tiger.

Hyper Criticism

Why did people insist on holding Tiger to a higher standard than other players? People thought that his natural ability meant he would always win, forgetting that was impossible. Fans also wanted to see Tiger set new records. Instead of measuring his performance against other players on the PGA Tour, they compared him to the greatest golfers of all time, such as Jack Nicklaus and Arnold Palmer.

Tiger had to learn how to deal with the constant public pressure that his incredible success had created. He worked with public

Best ever?: Tiger is slowly gaining on the records of golf greats Arnold Palmer *(left)* and Jack Nicklaus *(center)*.

relations specialists to control his emotions and promote a positive image as someone polite, professional, and above the fray. Some players on the tour found him a little cold. But others described him as friendly and outgoing. Everyone agreed on one thing—Tiger was extremely competitive, focused, and self-assured.

The endorsement and appearance deals that brought Tiger considerable wealth also brought many obligations. In return for the money, Tiger made commercials, attended meetings, and traveled to many places. At the same time, he continued to compete in tournaments. The demands on his time wore him down and left him tired. But when his dad tried to get him to slow down, Tiger just smiled. "You know me," he said. He had been an overachiever since childhood, and he wasn't about to change his ways.

> To help keep up with the demands of his endorsements and tour events, Tiger's sponsor NetJets offered him the use of a private plane. A small group of assistants keep him on a very tight schedule.

Tiger did find a way to ease some of the pressures of his life. He bought a townhouse in Isleworth, a luxury gated community in Orlando, Florida. The community has its own golf course, where he could practice and relax in privacy. Typically, Tiger competed in golf tournaments every other week, resting during the off week. He told visitors to his website that he liked to play with his computer in his downtime. He browsed on websites and even invested online.

Tiger also remained very close to both of his parents, even though they were living separately. Tiger's parents were visible and vocal supporters of their son. They attended every tournament. And every year, Kultida gave Tiger a new plush tiger head to use as a driver cover,

On course: Despite being separated, Tiger's parents continued to go to his tournaments and cheer him from the sidelines.

embroidered with the words "With Love, From Mom," in her native Thai language.

"I Finally Got It"

Beyond the money, appearances, schedules, parties, and media attention, there was one constant: Tiger Woods loved to play golf. As hard as practice could be, it was still fun. The only thing that wasn't fun was being in a slump.

Tiger went to work with Coach Harmon, breaking down his swing and analyzing what was going wrong. Tiger wanted to improve his accuracy without losing his great power. But as many athletes know, analyzing something can hamper performance. By breaking down the components of his swing, something that once seemed natural suddenly became something he had to think about. Yet, this difficult process led Tiger to his next breakthrough. As the 1999 PGA Tour began, Tiger's new swing was working. His accuracy improved. His drives stayed on the fairways more often, in good position for him to reach the green. Statistically, the difference was small, but the effect was huge.

"I finally got it," Tiger told his coach. "It all starts to feel natural to me." As his long game improved, so did his short game. Tiger's putting suddenly became deadly accurate. As 1999 continued, his slump ended with a bang.

Turnaround: Tiger encourages his putt to get in the hole at the 1999 Buick Invitational. He won the tournament and went on to have a great year.

Starting with the Buick Invitational, Tiger won eight events on the PGA Tour in 1999. He also finished second in one tournament and third in another, giving him top finishes in more than half of the PGA Tour tournaments that year. Eighteen times he landed in the top twenty-five, and sixteen times he was in the top ten. He made every cut (scored low enough to play all four rounds of a tournament). He won $6,616,585, far more than anyone else on the PGA Tour. It was the most dominating year for a golfer since Jack Nicklaus was in his prime. But 1999 was just a warm-up.

To get ready for the 2000 season, Tiger made several changes to Team Tiger, the group of coaches and professional managers around him. At the age of twenty-four, Tiger wanted to take more control of his decisions. He hired a new agent, Mark Steinberg. His new caddie, Steve Williams, was more low key than his previous one. Some observers said the changes were a sign that Tiger was becoming his own man, moving away from the advisers his father had helped him select. Or perhaps it was just the mark of a more self-assured, mature athlete. With his new team in place, the young superstar set out to see if he could go 1999 one better.

USA TODAY Snapshots®

Tiger vs. Golden Bear

Who golf course superintendents believe would win if Tiger Woods played Jack Nicklaus in his prime:

Tiger Woods
46.9%

Jack Nicklaus
41.1%

Source: Golf Course Superintendents Association of America

By April Umminger and Dave Merrill, USA TODAY © 2002

> Tiger underwent LASIK surgery in 1999. He was so nearsighted that his doctor had to be within one foot of his face before he could see how many fingers the doctor was holding up. After his surgery, Tiger's vision became 20/15. This meant Tiger could see more clearly at longer distances. (An object 20 feet away had the same clarity for Tiger that for other people was only clear at 15 feet away.)

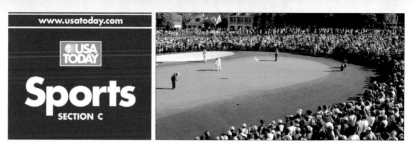
Woods, caddie part ways

From the Pages of
USA TODAY

Golf's favorite twosome is no more. Tiger Woods fired caddie Mike "Fluff" Cowan after 2 1/2 years.

The pair won seven PGA Tour events, including the 1997 Masters, which Woods said he couldn't have won without Cowan's calming help.

"I appreciate the support which Fluff has provided and recognize the contributions Fluff has made to my success as a professional," Woods said. "But it is time to move on, and I feel confident we will remain friends."

In a March *Golf Digest* interview, Cowan discussed his financial arrangement with Woods: $1,000 weekly and up to 10% of his winnings.

Cowan, 50, has caddied for Woods, 23, since he turned professional in August 1996. Before that, Cowan caddied for Peter Jacobsen for 19 years.

With Woods, Cowan became golf's best-known caddie. A Grateful Dead fan and 2-handicapper, he earned an estimated $165,000 last year. He has his own web site and appeared in a commercial.

Woods' new caddie is Steve Williams, who worked for Raymond Floyd for 12 years.

—Debbie Becker, March 9, 1999

Fluff Cowan

Grand Slam

There are four major events that golf fans and pros consider the most competitive and difficult: the Masters, the U.S. Open Championship, the British Open Championship, and the PGA Championship. Collectively, they are called the grand slam.

For decades, pro golfers dreamed of winning all four in the same year. But no one had ever done it. Ben Hogan came close in 1953, winning three of the four events. Jack Nicklaus and others have won two out of four in the same year.

In 2000 Tiger also dreamed of winning the grand slam. But in the first event, the Masters, he placed a disappointing fifth. That meant an official grand slam was out of the question. Yet Tiger didn't give up. In fact, his game caught fire that spring. He won both the U.S. and British Opens with impressive performances. But could he win three in one year?

Back to back: In 2000 Tiger won the U.S. Open *(left)* and the British Open *(right)*.

At the 2000 PGA Championship that August, the world watched to find out. This event was significant in many ways. Tiger was paired with Nicklaus for the first two rounds on the Valhalla Golf Course in Louisville, Kentucky—a course that Nicklaus, a noted golf course architect, had designed.

On the first day, Tiger shot a sizzling 66. But so did Scott Dunlap. On day two, Tiger shot a 67, just one stroke more than Dunlap. On the third day, Dunlap lost his lead, but fellow Californian Bob May, who shot a 66, was only one stroke behind Tiger. May had also been a promising amateur but had not done as well as a pro—until Valhalla. On the last day, May again shot a 66, while Tiger shot a 67. That meant May and Tiger were tied for first place. They would have to face each other in a three-hole playoff.

USA TODAY Snapshots®

Tiger roars to record scores

Tiger Woods tied his own record when he shot 18 under par in last year's PGA Championship. Lowest final scores in relation to par in the PGA Championship (since 1958[1]):

Tiger Woods	(2006, Medinah Country Club)	-18
Tiger Woods	(2000, Valhalla Golf Club)	-18
Steve Elkington	(1995, Riviera Country Club)	-17
David Toms	(2001, Atlanta Athletic Club)	-15
Lee Trevino	(1984, Shoal Creek Country Club)	-15

1 – Was a match-play event prior to 1958

Photo resource from Reuters

Source: pga.com   By Ellen J. Horrow and Bob Laird, USA TODAY © 2007

As May and Tiger began the playoff at hole sixteen, the fans went wild. "Is this what you get every week?" May asked Woods as the noise became overwhelming. "You got it," Tiger replied. Tiger birdied the hole with an incredible 7-iron shot that sailed more than 170 yards to the green. A twenty-foot putt gave him a one-shot lead. By the time they teed up for the last hole, Tiger, with a score of 7, still had a single stroke advantage over May.

On the final hole of the playoff, Tiger's drive went wide left, hit a golf cart, and bounced into trees. Yet the ball somehow found a decent lie in the grass! But two shots later, he ended up in a bunker. It looked as if Tiger would need at least three more shots to sink his ball. May found the green on his third shot, with his ball only sixty feet from the cup. He could easily two-putt the hole. The pressure was on.

Tiger walked toward the deep sand trap, disappeared from view, and sent his ball sailing out of the bunker. It flew toward the hole, stopping a mere eighteen inches from the cup. Tiger tapped it in. He had used only two shots for a total score of 12.

May had lost his advantage. Since he had already used eleven shots, he needed an incredibly long putt just to tie the game. He swung. The ball rolled toward the hole, closer, closer, closer—and stopped at the lip of the cup.

The crowd roared. Tiger's arm shot into the air to signal his victory. He had won three out of four events needed for the grand slam. He

PGA win: Tiger hugs Bob May after a grueling final round in the 2000 PGA Championship. The win gave Tiger the trophies for three out of the four major PGA Tour events in the same year. Only the legendary Ben Hogan had reached this pinnacle.

was only the second pro golfer ever to have done it. And he'd had golf's best season ever, by any measure.

Master Pressure

Over the next six months, there was a lot of speculation in the golf world about whether Tiger would win the 2001 Masters in April. And if he did, would that amount to a grand slam? Some said no, because all four events had to be won in the same calendar year. Others said yes, because Tiger would hold all the championships at the same time. But whether it was considered a grand slam or not, a fourth major title in a row would rank among the greatest sports achievements of all time.

Hype and excitement mixed as the contestants took their first swings at the 2001 Masters. Tiger struggled through the first round, while other young players, such as Chris DiMarco, caught fire. On the first day, DiMarco blistered the course, leading with a 7-under-par 65. Tiger's 70 left him far back in the pack. On day two, Woods played better, finishing in second place. But DiMarco stayed hot and continued in the lead at 10 under par.

Stage set: With three major wins in 2000, Tiger held the stage for an exciting 2001 Masters. Winning it would give him four majors in a row—a feat no golfer had ever achieved. Tiger and Chris DiMarco (*left*) were paired in the third round.

On day three, Tiger and DiMarco played together. They hung tough through the front nine, but Woods charged ahead relentlessly. He bird-ied the thirteenth hole, the fourteenth, and then made a short chip shot on the fifteenth to set up his third straight birdie. Tiger was in first place. DiMarco had dropped two strokes behind.

Meanwhile, Phil Mickelson, who had lost to Tiger many times in the past, had fought his way past DiMarco into second place. After spending his career chasing Tiger, Mickelson vowed to beat him in the Masters. "I desperately want this," he told a reporter for the Associated Press.

Round four: Phil Mickelson lines up a putt during the fourth round at the 2001 Masters.

Mickelson wouldn't win the Masters Tournament until 2004. By that time, Tiger had won the tournament three times.

For the Slam

On the fourth day, before a packed gallery of fans and millions of tele-vision viewers, Woods and Mickelson battled head-to-head for the Masters championship. With a one-stroke lead, Tiger approached the first tee boldly, sending a long drive down the fairway. Then it veered left, landing in the rough. Tiger bogied the first hole, losing his advan-tage. He and Mickelson were even.

In the meantime, another golfer, David Duval, had played so well that he had tied the other two men for the lead. The tournament had become a three-way contest. After the fifteenth hole, Tiger had a one-stroke lead. But he had a hard time on the challenging sixteenth hole, barely managing par. Mickelson had a chance to catch up, but the pressure affected him as well. His tee shot careened right, forcing a difficult putt that led to a bogey on the hole. It put Mickelson two strokes behind Tiger.

All eyes turned to Duval, playing ahead of Tiger. He was doing extremely well, keeping up with the leaders. But then Duval began to stumble ever so slightly. He missed a putt on the seventeenth hole and then again on the eighteenth. He finished with a 67 on the final round, for a total score of 274 in the tournament.

Starting the eighteenth hole, Tiger had a total score of 269. The hole was a par 4—all he had to do was make par, and he would beat Duval. But that was easier said than done. As he teed off at the eighteenth hole, Tiger sent a monster drive down the fairway—right into a bunker. The crowd fell silent. Tiger's caddie, Steve Williams, handed him a wedge. Tiger stared, swung, and sent the ball seventy-five yards. The ball rolled to a halt eighteen feet from the hole. It was close, but Tiger had missed easier putts. Every golfer had, especially here. The Masters has a history of breaking hearts with errant rolls a few feet, even a few inches, from victory.

Quiet challenger: David Duval made his move during the fourth round of the 2001 Masters.

Woods ignored history, the crowd, and everything but the ball. He swung. The ball hopped ahead, ducked slightly to the side, then back, back, back, and into the hole. He finished the tournament with 272 strokes, two better than Duval and three better than Mickelson.

Woods had not only won his second Masters, he had made his

April 10, 2001

Tiger's masterpiece captivates viewers

From the Pages of
USA TODAY

Tiger Woods continues to be a master of TV sports drama, but the golf world is going to have to get along without him for a few weeks.

Woods isn't expected to play the next 4 weeks. He'll likely be at the Byron Nelson Classic in Dallas on May 10-13, play in Germany a week later, then be back in the USA at The Memorial in Dublin, Ohio.

After that, his relentless pursuit of the majors continues with the U.S. Open in Tulsa, June 14-17; the British Open, July 19-22 at Royal Lytham and St. Anne's; and the PGA Championship, Aug. 16-19 in Duluth, Ga.

Woods' historic victory Sunday in Augusta at The Masters kept viewers glued to the set as he held off David Duval and Phil Mickelson.

When all the data is in, CBS is almost certain to end a 3-year slide in its 2-day Masters ratings.

Saturday's 7.8 preliminary national rating, the highest for a third round since 1972, was 32% higher than last year's 5.9.

"I thought in 1997 we had achieved an unsurpassable level," CBS Sports President Sean McManus said Monday. "It looks like nothing may be unsurpassable when it comes to Tiger Woods and The Masters."

own history. Commentators stopped debating whether his achievement was a grand slam or not. Instead, they found a new name for it—the Tiger Slam. As the ball nestled into the bottom of the hole, Tiger Woods froze on the green. He stared into space. Then he put his hand to his face and cried.

With Woods battling Augusta's storied grounds and his fourth consecutive major within reach, the final-round rating might rank with the all-time high 14.1 achieved for Woods' first Masters crown in 1997. The combined audience for the 2 days might top 50 million.

Ratings records were set in the three majors won by Woods last year—the British Open, U.S. Open and PGA Championship. Sunday's final Masters round presented further evidence of Woods becoming the most popular athlete in any sport.

"Like Michael Jordan did, Tiger has brought more fans to the sport and made the other players play better," said Jon Mandel of Mediacom. "And the fans appreciate it."

—Rudy Martzke, April 10, 2001

USA TODAY Snapshots®

Tiger aims low at Masters

Three-time Masters champion Tiger Woods has two of the lowest scores in Masters tournament history. The lowest scores through 72 holes:

	Score
Tiger Woods (1997)	**-18**
Jack Nicklaus (1965)	**-17**
Raymond Floyd (1976)	**-17**
Tiger Woods (2001)	**-16**

Source: www.masters.org   By Ellen J. Horrow and Karl Gelles, USA TODAY © 2005

New face: Fans wondered if Tiger could win back-to-back Masters. But they also wondered who was the woman with his mom on the sidelines. By the end of the opening round, viewers knew Tiger was introducing the world to his girlfriend, Elin Nordegren.

Life as the Master

As the date of the 2002 Masters tournament at Augusta National Golf Club came closer, the golf world wondered if Tiger Woods could win the Masters twice in a row. But on the first day of the tournament, the media was asking a more personal question: who was the pretty blonde sitting next to Tiger's mom in the stands?

Elin Nordegren of Sweden was making her first public appearance as Tiger's new girlfriend. Actually, the two had been quietly dating since they met at the 2001 British Open at Royal Lytham, when Elin was working as a nanny for Swedish golfer Jesper Parnevik. When she showed up at the Masters, everyone was curious—and worried.

In the sports world, many fans don't like it when great athletes fall in love. They often blame girlfriends and wives for distracting athletes from concentrating on the game. People wondered the same thing about Tiger's new girlfriend.

Breaking New Records

As it turned out, fans had more to worry about than Elin's presence. The Augusta golf course had been lengthened by 238 yards and redesigned to make it more challenging. The weather was terrible.

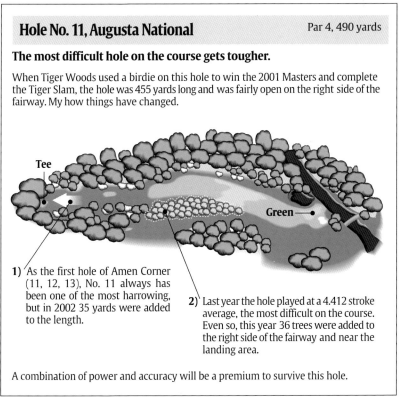

Hole No. 11, Augusta National
Par 4, 490 yards

The most difficult hole on the course gets tougher.

When Tiger Woods used a birdie on this hole to win the 2001 Masters and complete the Tiger Slam, the hole was 455 yards long and was fairly open on the right side of the fairway. My how things have changed.

Tee

Green

1) As the first hole of Amen Corner (11, 12, 13), No. 11 always has been one of the most harrowing, but in 2002 35 yards were added to the length.

2) Last year the hole played at a 4.412 stroke average, the most difficult on the course. Even so, this year 36 trees were added to the right side of the fairway and near the landing area.

A combination of power and accuracy will be a premium to survive this hole.

Source: USA TODAY

By Robert W. Ahrens, USA TODAY

All wet: Fans whipped out their umbrellas as heavy rains made the 2002 Masters course into a slushy mess. Yet Tiger won the tournament and his third green jacket.

On the first day, the course was so wet and sloppy that players found their shoes, golf clubs, and balls slick with mud. On the second day, only half the players finished all eighteen holes before heavy rains began. This group included Vijay Singh, who had won the 2000 Masters and was leading the pack. The other golfers, including Tiger, had to stop playing after the tenth hole. Heavy rain canceled the third day of play—shortening the tournament from four rounds to three.

On Sunday, the final day, Tiger woke up early to run four miles, part of his routine to keep fit. Then he went to the slippery golf course to finish the last eight holes of his second round. With no time for rest, Woods started the final round six strokes behind Singh—a big lead to overcome, even in perfect weather.

The sun came out during the final round, but it was too late to dry up the golf course. Puddles were everywhere. The other players began to fall apart. Even Singh, the leader, fell two strokes behind Tiger when his mud-caked ball landed in the water. Amazingly, Woods seemed to almost enjoy the horrible conditions. He played a steady game and emerged as the winner. As Tiger slipped his arms into the coveted green jacket and turned to acknowledge his screaming fans, he made history as the third player ever to have won two Masters tournaments in a row.

The 2002 season proved that Tiger was in a class by himself. He not only broke old records, he set new ones. He was the first player to win the Byron Nelson Award and the Vardon Trophy four years in a row. He was the first to lead the U.S. Open twice from start to finish without being tied at the end of any round. He finished the year with 176 consecutive weeks as the number one player in the Official World Golf Ranking and was named PGA Tour Player of the Year. And he was still just twenty-six years old.

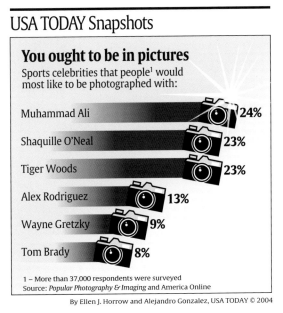

USA TODAY Snapshots

You ought to be in pictures
Sports celebrities that people[1] would most like to be photographed with:

Muhammad Ali — 24%
Shaquille O'Neal — 23%
Tiger Woods — 23%
Alex Rodriguez — 13%
Wayne Gretzky — 9%
Tom Brady — 8%

1 – More than 37,000 respondents were surveyed
Source: *Popular Photography & Imaging* and America Online

By Ellen J. Horrow and Alejandro Gonzalez, USA TODAY © 2004

Good Luck Turns . . .

Tiger remained one of the top competitors on the PGA Tour in 2003 and 2004. But he couldn't seem to win a PGA Tour event. Fans said he was in another slump. When Vijay Singh won the 2004 Deutsche Bank Championship in Norton, Massachusetts, he replaced Tiger as the world's number one. Journalists concluded that Tiger had lost his touch. They thought his best days were over.

If you ain't got that swing

With Tiger Woods' swing troubles this year come the worst driving accuracy statistics of his career. He is hitting fairways less than 60% of the time. At the height of his career, he was over 70%.

At the U.S. Open, accuracy is at a premium. The rough at its deepest will be 4 inches tall, and the fairways are dauntingly narrow at Shinnecock Hills, this year's tournament site on Long Island, N.Y.

Sixth hole
Par 4, 474 yards

Perhaps Woods' greatest concern should be the sixth hole, which played as the most difficult the last time the U.S. Open was at Shinnecock in 1995. It played to a stroke average of 4.41.

The hole contains the only water hazards on the course, and players will tee off into a blind landing zone.

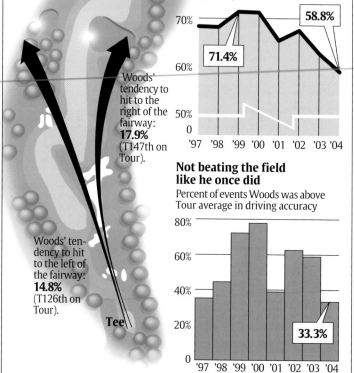

AP

Off target: Woods' driver has failed him in 2004.

Woods' tendency to hit to the right of the fairway:
17.9%
(T147th on Tour).

Woods' tendency to hit to the left of the fairway:
14.8%
(T126th on Tour).

Tee

Woods' driving accuracy percentage through the years:

58.8%

71.4%

70%

60%

50%

0

'97 '98 '99 '00 '01 '02 '03 '04

Not beating the field like he once did

Percent of events Woods was above Tour average in driving accuracy

80%

60%

40%

20%

33.3%

0

'97 '98 '99 '00 '01 '02 '03 '04

Sources: USA TODAY research; data provided by SHOT**Link**   By Julie Snider, USA TODAY

Tiger saw it differently. He was busy remaking himself into a better golfer. He didn't mind losing some tournaments in order to develop new skills that would help him play golf well for years to come. In fact, he realized that if he didn't do things differently than he had before, he might not be able to play golf for very much longer. His swing put a lot of strain on his right knee, which had to be repaired by surgery.

During this time, Tiger was also developing his relationship with Elin Nordegren. They were compatible on a number of levels. Elin is very competitive, as is Tiger. She's devoted to physical fitness, which is a personal philosophy that Tiger preaches and practices. She enjoys a variety of sports, as both spectator and participant. In addition, she seemed to handle the media's attention well. After the U.S. team won the Presidents Cup in November of 2003, the couple celebrated with a safari vacation at a South African game reserve. One evening, during a sunset walk, Tiger asked Elin to marry him. She said yes.

Happy couple: Tiger and his fiancée, Elin, cheered on Stanford's basketball team in 2004.

A Private Affair

When you are as famous as Tiger Woods, keeping things a secret isn't easy. How could Tiger stop celebrity chasers and reporters from turning his private wedding into a public event? Tiger did it by cleverly holding the wedding a thousand miles away from the United States on a tiny island in the middle of the Caribbean Sea.

On October 5, 2004, Tiger and Elin were married at a private golf resort on the island of Barbados. They reserved all the resort's 112 rooms, the golf course, and the clubhouse, so only invited guests and family would be there. To stop photographers from flying over the ceremony and snapping pictures, Tiger hired the island's only helicopter charter company for the day. Instead of flying to their wedding on Tiger's private plane, which might attract the attention of reporters, Tiger and Elin sailed there on their new yacht, which they named *Privacy*. The golf course setting made Tiger feel right at home. After the ceremony, there was dinner in the clubhouse, dancing in a tent

Love boat: Tiger and Elin spent their honeymoon on their yacht, named *Privacy*. They scuba dived, swam, and relaxed after their wedding in October 2004.

erected on the course, and a brilliant display of fireworks in the evening. Tiger and Elin spent their honeymoon scuba diving, spear fishing, swimming, and relaxing on their yacht, enjoying their private time together.

> Tiger's 155-foot yacht, named *Privacy,* has three decks. It looks more like an ocean liner than a boat and needs a large space to dock. The 6,500-square-foot interior includes six staterooms, a theater, and a gym.

A Thrilling Season

A win at the Buick Invitational in January 2005 set the pace for a thrilling comeback season for Tiger. By March 6, after winning against Phil Mickelson at the Ford Championship in Miami, Florida, Tiger was once again rated number one on the Official World Golf Ranking. And he wasn't just winning, he was making the kind of impossible shots that thrilled fans and made golf history.

One of those shots came during the 2005 Masters tournament. Tiger had one of the worst starts of his career, making five bogeys in

Another Buick: Tiger started off his 2005 PGA Tour season with his third win at the Buick Invitational.

the first thirteen holes to fall seven strokes behind the leader, Chris DiMarco.

Then, on the six-teenth hole of the final round, Tiger's ball landed at the edge of the rough, about thir-ty feet downhill from the hole. He slowly paced the steeply sloped green, scop-ing out the distance and noting the hazard of a nearby bunker. Commentators pre-dicted Tiger would have to aim for a spot many yards above the hole. But Woods chipped the ball aggressively, sending it rolling gently along the rising slope. It curved perfectly to-ward the hole. The murmurs of astounded fans rose in pitch as Tiger's ball inched closer to the hole, then hovered dramatically at the lip for a split second before falling in.

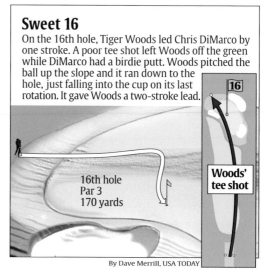

Sweet 16

On the 16th hole, Tiger Woods led Chris DiMarco by one stroke. A poor tee shot left Woods off the green while DiMarco had a birdie putt. Woods pitched the ball up the slope and it ran down to the hole, just falling into the cup on its last rotation. It gave Woods a two-stroke lead.

16th hole
Par 3
170 yards

Woods' tee shot

By Dave Merrill, USA TODAY

Augusta National's sixteenth is a par 3 hole called Redbud. To get to the green, a player has to hit a shot over a long stretch of water. Three bunkers create further hazards around a heavily sloped green.

The fans roared. Tiger and his caddie high-fived. Tiger was two strokes ahead and won the tournament in high spirits. Slipping on the green jacket for the fourth time in his career, Tiger dedicated the win

High five: Caddie Steve Williams and Tiger high-five after his amazing chip shot on the sixteenth at the 2005 Masters. The birdie put him in the lead for a fourth green jacket.

to his dad, who was fighting prostate cancer. "He couldn't come out to the course to enjoy this," Tiger told his fans, adding, "He was with me every step of the way."

That year Tiger had other incredible wins. On Father's Day, he won the British Open for a second time. This time Tiger won the Claret Jug, the first prize of the British Open, by five strokes over his nearest competitor. Tiger also finished second in the U.S. Open and won six total PGA Tour events, plus two tournaments at the World Golf Championships for one of his best years yet. He dedicated all of his

Kissing the Claret Jug: Tiger celebrates his win at the 2005 British Open with a kiss of the Claret Jug.

wins to his father, fearing his dad would not be around much longer to share his triumphs.

Doing It for Dad

Coming off his amazing season, Tiger seemed to be unstoppable at the start of 2006. Excitement was high as he won the Buick Invitational for the second straight time in January. But then he lost the WGC Accenture Match Play Championship by one stroke and lost the Players Championship in March by seven strokes.

August 17, 2006

Imagine there's no Tiger

From the Pages of
USA TODAY

Just imagine the last decade of pro golf without Tiger Woods.

Woods' presence has translated into a wonderful life for the PGA Tour with greater TV dollars and resulting larger purses.

"I thank him all the time for it because he deserves it, not just for the purses but the interest in the game of golf," Phil Mickelson says. "Because that leads to increased revenue opportunities off the course, companies that wouldn't be interested in golf he's helped bring to the game. So it's been beneficial for every player out here, myself included."

Where would the PGA Tour be if Woods had picked up a football at age 3 instead of a 5-iron?

"You would have had two or three guys who would have been better known," says Neal Pilson, a sports television consultant. "Would the ratings have been as high? Probably not."

PGA Tour Commissioner Tim Finchem credits Woods for short-term and long-term effects.

"The reason he has such impact is not only his skill but his persona and the way he carries himself. He's the most recognized athlete on the planet," Finchem says. "He drives TV ratings, brings more people out to the tournaments and creates more media coverage.

"His long-term impact has yet to be defined. I believe it will be that he changed the face of the game. He's attracting so many kids who haven't had access to golf. He's giving the game a broader appeal, especially from the ethnic and race perspective. I think he'll change the game globally. That may be his finest accomplishment."

—Jim Halley and Jerry Potter, August 17, 2006

Fans hoped he would make a comeback at the Masters in April. Tiger performed brilliantly off each tee, driving long and accurately. When he did hit a bunker, Tiger recovered with more amazing uphill chip shots. But his putting was a real problem. Often he needed three strokes to sink the ball, while his competitors used only one or two. Tiger finished third.

"It was the best I've hit in years," Tiger said at his news conference later. "But then again I absolutely lost it out there on the greens. I putted so bad. I'm going to probably go snap this putter in about eight pieces," he joked.

After the tournament, Tiger flew home to spend time with his father, who was very ill. His dad died three weeks later, on May 3, 2006. Earl Woods was seventy-four years old. Tiger, Elin, and his mother greeted more than two hundred family members and friends at a private service. Afterward, Tiger was so broken hearted he couldn't bear

Saying good-bye: Elin, Tiger, and Kultida go to a memorial reception after the burial of Earl Woods. Tiger's father died after a long battle with cancer in May 2006.

to pick up a golf club for a month. He didn't get back into the game until nine weeks later—a long time in the fast-paced world of pro golf. He played badly in the U.S. Open. For the first time as a pro, he missed the cut at a major championship.

> Until the 2006 U.S. Open, Tiger had made the cut in thirty-nine consecutive majors.

New Beginnings

If the 2006 U.S. Open had been one of the lowest points in Tiger's career, his victory at the British Open a month later was one of the highest. His performance was masterly, with accurate and controlled strokes on every hole. He finished with a two-stroke victory over Chris DiMarco. It was the third time Tiger had won the British Open. On the eighteenth green of the final round, Tiger tapped in his ball, smiling broadly. With tears in his eyes, he embraced Steve, then Elin, and then each of the members of his training team. With his mother watching from home, it was the first time at least one of his parents had not been there to see his victory. "All these emotions just came pouring out," Tiger said, "and all the

Bouncing back: After abysmal play at the 2006 U.S. Open, Tiger bounced back with a bang at the British Open. His caddie comforts Tiger after an emotional win that brought forth tears and memories of his dad.

things that my father has meant to me and the game of golf, I just wish he could have seen it one more time."

For the rest of 2006, Tiger seemed unbeatable. He won each of the next six PGA Tour tournaments with lower and lower scores and larger and larger margins over his competitors. In August Tiger won his fiftieth PGA Tour title with a three-stroke victory over Jim Furyk in the Buick Open. He won the PGA Championship two weeks later with a five-stroke victory. He ended the season with an eight-stroke victory in the WCG-American Express Championship.

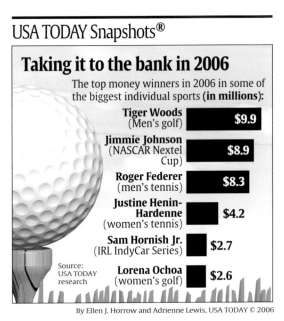

USA TODAY Snapshots®

Taking it to the bank in 2006

The top money winners in 2006 in some of the biggest individual sports **(in millions):**

Tiger Woods (Men's golf)	$9.9
Jimmie Johnson (NASCAR Nextel Cup)	$8.9
Roger Federer (men's tennis)	$8.3
Justine Henin-Hardenne (women's tennis)	$4.2
Sam Hornish Jr. (IRL IndyCar Series)	$2.7
Lorena Ochoa (women's golf)	$2.6

Source: USA TODAY research

By Ellen J. Horrow and Adrienne Lewis, USA TODAY © 2006

Tiger has become close friends with tennis superstar Roger Federer. They've appeared in ads together—both have Nike endorsements—as well as going to each other's major events.

But Tiger has always said that his family and charitable projects have meant as much to him as winning golf tournaments. One of the proudest days of his life was when he opened the Tiger Woods Learning Center in Anaheim, California. The thirty-five-thousand-

Grand tour: Tiger Woods smiles as students at the Tiger Woods Learning Center show former president Bill Clinton some of their high-tech equipment. The center, opened in 2006, helps thousands of students in Southern California explore careers in science, math, and technology.

square-foot facility offers thousands of kids a chance to explore career paths in science, math, and technology using state-of-the art computer and lab equipment. Another learning center is being planned for the Washington, D.C., area.

Fatherhood and the Future

On his thirty-first birthday, Tiger posted a message on his website to share one more piece of good news with his fans. He and Elin were expecting their first child in the summer of 2007. "Obviously, we couldn't be happier and our families are thrilled," Tiger wrote. "I have always wanted to be a dad. I just wish my father could be around to share the experience."

Before the birth, Tiger had said if the choice was between being with his wife during the birth or missing a major, there'd be no contest—the baby was it! But when the doctor told his wife to go into the hospital early, Woods was still playing in the U.S. Open.

Tiger wanted to fly home in the middle of the tournament, but his wife urged him to continue and get a "W"—a win—for the family. He finished second, then hopped on a plan and went straight to the hospital, where his daughter Sam Alexis was born the day after Father's Day.

"That night was infinitely more rewarding than any "W" ever could have been," Tiger told reporters later. He couldn't resist putting a golf club into his daughter's tiny hand. "She couldn't quite hold it," Woods admitted. "But it was there."

Tiger and his wife decided to name their daughter Sam because his father had always called him that. "He rarely ever called me Tiger," he explained. "I would ask him, 'Why don't you ever call me Tiger?' He says, 'Well, you look more like a Sam.'"

The new father rearranged his busy schedule and decided not to attend the Buick Open so he could spend time with his wife and new daughter. But he was back to play in the final seven PGA tournaments that year, winning four of them. Baby Sam and Elin even came to cheer him on for his thirteenth major win at the 2007 PGA Championship.

It was an exciting time for Tiger in another way. Two golf courses he designed for resorts in North Carolina and the United Arab Emirates in the Middle East were in the first stages of being built. And in January 2008, he announced plans to open a new Tiger Woods Learning Center in Washington, D.C., continuing his father's legacy of inspiring children to reach for their dreams.

On January 21, Martin Luther King Day, the entire family gathered at the learning center in California to dedicate an eight-foot-high bronze statue of Tiger with his arm around his dad. The inscription on the statue reads: "I challenge you to make a difference in the world, to reach higher and farther than you ever imagined."

www.usatoday.com

USA TODAY

Sports

SECTION C

August 15, 2007

Woods will design U.S. course

From the Pages of
USA TODAY

TRAVELERS REST, SC -- Tiger Woods is moving methodically toward Jack Nicklaus' record of 18 victories in major championships, but he's not interested in challenging Nicklaus for supremacy in golf course design.

"I always wanted to be in the design business," Woods said Tuesday while announcing his first project in the USA. "He's done over 200. I'll do only one or two at any time."

Woods, who earned his 13th major title at the PGA Championship on Sunday, expects to add projects gradually in a schedule that includes new daughter Sam Alexis.

He arrived in this mountain community near the North Carolina-South Carolina border Tuesday morning to join Jim Anthony, founder and president of The Cliffs Communities, to announce his design project in the Blue Ridge Mountain area of Swannanoa, N.C.

Anthony had drawings of a golf course Woods mapped out at age 11. "I don't believe there's any golfer that has more desire," Anthony said. "He takes us to another level."

"I really can't mess this up," Woods said. "It's an amazing piece of property."

Woods described the site as bowl-shaped and rolling, with a view of seven mountain ranges. It's different from his first design, in the deserts of Dubai, where the contours had to be created.

"It's just sitting there," Woods said of this mountain property. "All you have to do is put a golf course on it."

That could take as long as two years. Woods already is trying to determine the configuration of the holes, but he said he has so many options that it's difficult to decide. It will have one characteristic: It's designed for walking.

"Jim and I both have an interest in fitness," Woods said. "Obesity and diabetes is an epidemic in the country. We want something to encourage physical fitness."

—Jerry Potter, August 15, 2007

All smiles: Tiger delights in his daughter, Sam, held by his mother, who stands next to Elin. They are at the unveiling of a statue of Earl and Tiger at the learning center in early 2008.

Tiger Woods has tied or beaten every record in the game of golf, except one. He needs just five more major tournament victories to tie Jack Nicklaus's record of eighteen major wins. When he does that—and nearly everyone believes he will someday—Tiger will be golf's greatest champion.

TIGER'S CAREER HIGHLIGHTS ... SO FAR

In a career with so many high points, it's hard to come up with a definitive list. Here's a sampling of how Tiger became a household name.

1991–1993: youngest champion ever to win three U.S. Junior Amateur Championships back-to-back

1994–1996: youngest champion to win three U.S. Amateur Championships back-to-back

1996: turned pro in August and won two events; named Sports Illustrated Sportsman of the Year at the age of twenty

1997: won his first Masters by a record twelve strokes; set a record by winning five PGA events in the first sixteen tournaments; ranked number one for the first time, the youngest ever to win the honor; named PGA Player of the Year

2000: won three of four grand slam majors: the U.S. Open, the British Open, and the PGA Championship

2001: won his second Masters: is the first to hold championships in all four majors simultaneously

2003: first to win the Jack Nicklaus Award, Byron Nelson Award, Vardon Trophy, and PGA Tour Player of the Year award five years in a row

2004: set a record with 264 consecutive weeks as number one player on the Official World Golf Ranking

2005: won his fourth Masters (tying Arnold Palmer but still two behind Jack Nicklaus), first player to win PGA Tour Player of the Year award seven times

2006: won British Open for third time and was named PGA Tour Player of the Year

2007: won the PGA Championship for the third time, named PGA Tour Player of the Year for the ninth time

2008: set new records for total career wins and the most career earnings of any player in PGA Tour history

GLOSSARY

address: the point at which the golfer takes his or her stance and prepares to swing the club

backswing: the motion of a golfer's hands, arms, and body as he or she pulls the club back before hitting the ball. The backswing creates the power for the shot.

birdie: a score that is one shot lower than par on a hole

bogey: a score that is one shot higher than par on a hole

bunker: a small depression on a fairway or next to a green, usually filled with sand. If filled with sand, it is also called a sand trap.

caddie: the person who carries a golfer's bag and keeps track of distances and conditions. When asked, the caddie offers the golfer advice and encouragement.

caddie

chip shot: a short, easy shot. It can be to the green from the fairway or from the woods to an area back in play.

chunking: when a golfer erroneously hits the ground with the clubhead before it strikes the ball

cup: the actual hole on the green into which the ball is hit

cut: the highest score a player can have at a tournament and still be allowed to play all four rounds of golf

divot: a piece of turf dug up by a golf swing. Players are expected to replace divots immediately.

divot

double bogey: a score that is two shots higher than par on a hole

drive: the first shot hit by a golfer on each hole

driving range: an area where golfers practice their swings and drives. These practice areas usually have distance markers, allowing the golfers to see how far they have hit their ball.

eagle: a score that is two shots lower than par on a hole

handicap: the average number of strokes over par a golfer normally plays. The lower the handicap, the better the golfer. The handicap is

drive

subtracted from the final score to see who wins. This system is used so that players of different abilities can compete against one another. Professional competitions do not use handicaps.

hazards: anything in the area of play that can make playing more difficult for a golfer. Bunkers are common hazards, but natural features, such as rocks or trees, can also be hazards.

hazards

head: the end of the golf club that hits the ball. The face is the surface that actually strikes the golf ball. The shape and size of the head varies with the type of club.

hook shot: a drive that curves from right to left while in the air. This curving action often puts the ball into a difficult area to play.

iron: a metal club with a grooved, angled head. The angle allows a golfer to give a shot loft.

iron game: shots made with irons. This term usually refers to the middle of each hole, after a drive from the tee.

lie of the ball: where the ball stops. A good lie means that a ball is placed well for the next shot to the green or the cup.

loft: the height of a golf shot

par: the number of shots a golfer is expected to use to complete a hole

pitch shot: a short, high-angle shot made with an iron and often used to get on the green or avoid a hazard

putt: a stroke used on the green, designed to roll the ball into the cup. Putts can be deceptively difficult.

reading the green: trying to determine how a ball will travel on the green. The slope of the green and other factors, such as the wind, make this critical step difficult on most putts.

reading the green

tee: a small wooden or plastic T-shaped peg, used to elevate the golf ball to make it easier to hit. The tee is used only at the start of each hole.

teeing off: taking the first shot on each hole. The golfer puts the ball on a tee before hitting it. The golfer may place the tee and the ball anywhere on the tee box, or marked area at the start of the hole. Two markers usually designate the tee box. There are often different tee boxes for men, women, and young golfers.

teeing off

wood: a club with a large head and a flat face, which allows a golfer to drive the ball very far. The heads of these clubs were originally made of wood. In modern times, metals are generally used.

SOURCES

5   John Strege, *Tiger* (New York: Broadway Books, 1997), 11.

7   Earl Woods with Fred Mitchell, *Playing Through* (New York: HarperCollins, 1998), 36.*

7   Ibid., 37.

11 Earl Woods with Fred Mitchell, *Playing Through*, 61.

12 Tim Rosaforte, *Tiger Woods—The Makings of a Champion* (New York: St. Martin's Press, 1997), 17.

17 Earl Woods with Fred Mitchell, *Playing Through*, 102.

18 Associated Press, "Woods Doesn't Want to Be Called African-American," April 22, 1997, *reporternews.com*, available online at http://www.texnews.com/tiger/race042297.html (April 1, 2008).

18 Tiger Woods statement, n.d., http://www.cbs.sportsline.com/u/fans/celebrity/tiger/about/quotes.html (April 1, 2008).

18 Strege, 16.

19 Tiger Woods, foreword to *Training a Tiger*, by Earl Woods with Pete McDaniel (New York: HarperCollins, 1997), xi.

19 Earl Woods with Fred Mitchell, *Playing Through*, 104.

20 Earl Woods with Pete McDaniel, *Training a Tiger*, 160.

21 Rosaforte, *Tiger Woods*, 23.

23 Earl Woods, "Tiger Quotes," *Official Website for Tiger Woods*, n.d., http://www.tigerwoods.com/defaultflash.sps (April 4, 2008).

25 Earl Woods with Fred Mitchell, *Playing Through*, 88.**

27 Strege, 71.

27 Ibid., 75.

28 Ibid., 76.

29 Rosaforte, *Tiger Woods*, 82.

30 Ibid.

30 Ibid., ix.

33 Earl Woods with Fred Mitchell, *Playing Through*, 116.

*There are several ways to spell Phong's name. This book uses the spelling that was adopted after the deceased South Vietnamese colonel's family was located.

**Earl's account differs slightly from the actual recorded scorecard of the event, which this book relies on for its description.

33 Strege, 82.

33 Ibid.

35–36 Ibid., 89.

36 Tiger Woods, "Athletes—Tiger Woods through the Years" *bio.video*, http://www.biography.com/broadband/main.do?video=bio-tiger-woods-threequestions (April 4, 2008).

39 Strege, 157.

42 Rosaforte, *Tiger Woods*, 165.

43 Ibid., 169.

46 Strege, 195.

46 Rosaforte, *Tiger Woods*, 183.

46 John Feinstein, *The First Coming—Tiger Woods: Master or Martyr* (New York: Ballantine Publishing Group, 1998), 45.

48 Strege, 205.

48 Rosaforte, *Tiger Woods*, 5.

55 Tim Rosaforte, *Raising the Bar* (New York: Thomas Dunne Books, 2000), 129.

55 Ibid.

55 John Feinstein, *The Majors* (New York: Little, Brown & Company, 1999), 22.

56 Rosaforte, *Raising the Bar*, 129.

57 Jack Nicklaus with Ken Bowden, *Jack Nicklaus: My Story* (New York: Simon & Schuster, 1997), 414.

57 *Tiger Woods: Heart of a Champion*, VHS, (Intersport, 2000).

57 Tiger Woods with the editors of Golf Digest, *How I Play Golf* (New York: Warner Books, 2001), 268.

58 Jay Brunza, quoted at http://www.cbs.sportsline.com/u/fans/celebrity/tiger/about/quotes.html/ accessed via Frontiernet.net (March 2, 2001).

59 Feinstein, *The Majors*, 149.

59 Rosaforte, *Raising the Bar*, xi.

59–60 Rosaforte, *Tiger Woods*, 235.

61 Tom Callahan, Associated Press, "Real Tiger Died in Vietnam Camp," September 14, 1997.

61 Ibid.

63–64 Rosaforte, *Raising the Bar*, 140.

65 Earl Woods, *Playing Through*, 191.

67   Rosaforte, *Raising the Bar*, 140.

71   Howard Richman, Knight Ridder, "Woods Wins PGA Championship in Playoff with May," August 21, 2000, available online at *reporternews.com*, http://www.texnews.com/tiger/winn0821.html (n.d.).

74   Jim Litke, Associated Press, "Mickelson to Face Major Crossroads in Final Round," April 7, 2001.

87   Mark Soltau, "Tiger Beats DiMarco in Playoff to Capture His Fourth Green Jacket," *Official Website for Tiger Woods*, April 11, 2005, www .http://tigerwoods.com (April 1, 2008).

90   Mark Soltau, "Hot Putter Helps Woods Score Comeback Win at the Buick Invitational," *Official Website for Tiger Woods*, January 14, 2005, http://www.tigerwoods.com/defaultflash.sps?page =fullstorynews&iNewsID=144592&categoryID=&pagenumber =1&cat=0 (April 1, 2008).

91–92   Mark Soltau, "Tiger Captures Third British Open and 11th Major Championship." *Official Website for Tiger Woods*, July 23, 2006, http://www.tigerwoods.com/defaultflash.sps (April 4, 2008).

93   Tiger Woods, "Excited Tiger, Elin to Become First-Time Parents This Summer," *Official Website for Tiger Woods*, December 30, 2006, http://www.tigerwoods.com (April 1, 2008).

95   Tiger Woods, "Tiger Woods Press Conference: AT&T National, Tuesday July 3, 2007," *Official Website for Tiger Woods*, July 3, 2007, http://www.tigerwoods.com/defaultflash.sps (April 4, 2008).

95   Ibid.

95   Ibid.

95   Mark Soltau, "Tiger and Earl's Fist Pump," *GolfDigest.com*, January 22, 2008, http://www.golfdigest.com/magazine/blogs/ localknowledge/2008/01/tiger-and-earls.html (April 3, 2008).

SELECTED BIBLIOGRAPHY

Anderson, Dave. "Why Woods Hasn't Won: His Putting." *New York Times*, February 7, 2001.

Brown, Clifton. "For Love, Fast Start Means Bigger Finish." *New York Times*, February 5, 2001.

——. "Gogel Sets Poppy Hills Mark and Leaves Past Behind." *New York Times*, February 3, 2001.

——. "At Pebble Beach, Singh Seeks His Day After Two Close Calls." *New York Times*, February 4, 2001.

——. "Woods Injures Knee After Collision with a Fan." *New York Times*, February 1, 2001.

Dahlbert, Tim. Associated Press. "Only Question for Woods May Be How He Wins Majors." August 21, 2000. Available online at *reporternews*, http://www.texnews.com/tiger/how0821.html (April 1, 2008).

Ebert, Jon. Scripps Howard News Service. "Tiger Doesn't Make Great Golf Courses Obsolete." April 29, 1997. Available online at *reporternews*, http://www.texnews.com/tiger/obso042997.html (April 1, 2008).

Feinstein, John. *The First Coming—Tiger Woods: Master or Martyr?* New York: Ballantine Publishing Group, 1998.

——. *The Majors.* New York: Little, Brown & Company, 1999.

Ferguson, Doug. Associated Press. "Tiger Gets a Fight, but Wins PGA." August 21, 2000. Available online at *reporternews*, http://www.texnews.com/tiger/fight0821.html (April 1, 2008).

Garner, Joe, and Bob Costas, et al. *And the Fans Roared: The Sports Broadcasts That Kept Us on the Edge of Our Seats.* CD. Naperville, IL: Sourcebooks, 2000.

Graffis, Herb. *The PGA.* New York: Thomas Y. Crowell Company, 1975.

Gola, Hank. "Epic Victory for Woods." *New York Daily News*, August 21, 2000.

Golf Magazine, "Seen & Heard." January 2001.

Juliano, Joe. Knight Ridder. "Tiger Woods Wins Masters in Memorable Fashion." April 14, 1997. Available online at *reporternews*, http://www.texnews.com/tiger/enor041497.html (April 1, 2008).

Nicklaus, Jack, with Ken Bowden. *Jack Nicklaus: My Story.* New York: Simon & Schuster, 1997.

Posanski, Joe. "Woods Gives Us a Closer Look." Knight Ridder News Service. August 21, 2000. Available online at *reporternews*, http://www.texnews.com/tiger/look0821.html (April 1, 2008).

Reagan, Danny. "The Impact Tiger Is Going to Make." Abilene Reporter-News. April 26, 1997. Available online at *reporternews*, http://www.texnews.com/tiger/dr042697.html (April 1, 2008).

Richman, Howard. "Woods Wins PGA Championship in Playoff with May." Knight Ridder News Service. August 21, 2000. Available online at *reporternews*, http://www.texnews.com/tiger/winn0821.html (April 1, 2008).

Rosaforte, Tim. *Raising the Bar.* New York: St. Martin's Press, 2000.

Sherman, Ed. "Tiger Woods Plays Golf with Michael Jordan, Tapes Oprah Winfrey Show." Chicago Tribune. April 22, 1997. Available online at *reporternews*, http://www.texnews.com/tiger/mike042297.html (April 1, 2008).

Sinnette, Calvin H. *Forbidden Fairways: A History of African Americans and the Game of Golf.* Chelsea, MI: Sleeping Bear Press, 1998.

Tiger Woods: Heart of a Champion. VHS. Intersport, 2000.

Timms, Ed, and Thomas G. Watts. "Multiracial Issues for Others Raised with Hoopla Surrounding Tiger Woods." Dallas Morning News. April 21, 1997. Available online at *reporternews*, http://www.texnews.com/tiger/multi042197.html (April 1, 2008).

Townsend, Brad. "After Masters Win, Some Wonder if Woods Can Hit the Grand Slam." Dallas Morning News. April 17, 1997. Available online at *reporternews*, http://www.texnews.com/tiger/slam041797.html (April 1, 2008).

Wiren, Gary. *The PGA Manual of Golf.* New York: MacMillan Publishing Company, 1991.

Woods, Earl, with Pete McDaniel. *Training a Tiger.* New York: HarperCollins, 1997.

Woods, Earl, with Fred Mitchell. *Playing Through.* New York: HarperCollins, 1998.

Woods, Earl, with Shari Lesser Wenk and the Tiger Woods Foundation. *Start Something.* New York: Simon & Schuster, 2000.

Woods, Tiger. *How I Play Golf.* New York: Warner Books, 2001.

"Woods Doesn't Want to Be Called African-American." Associated Press. April 22, 1997. Available online at *reporternews,* http://www.texnews. com/tiger/race042297.html (April 1, 2008).

FURTHER READING AND WEBSITES

Books

Andrisani, John. *Think Like a Tiger: An Analysis of Tiger Woods' Mental Game.* New York: Putnam, 2002.

Barrett, Ted. *Golf, a History.* London: Carlton Publishing Group, 2005.

Callahan, Tom. *In Search of Tiger: A Journey through Golf with Tiger Woods.* New York: Three Rivers Press, 2004.

Doeden, Matt. *Tiger Woods.* Minneapolis: Twenty-First Century Books, 2005.

McCord, Gary. *Golf for Dummies.* Riverside, NJ: Andrew McMeel Publishing, 2007.

Sampson, Curt. *Chasing Tiger.* London: Atria, 2004.

Time. *GOLF Magazine: The Best Instruction Book Ever.* Minneapolis: Twenty-First Century Books, 2008.

Websites

The Official Site of the Masters Golf Tournament
http://www.masters.org
This website provides information on the Masters Tournament, as well as videos, quizzes, and interviews.

Official Site of the PGA Tour
http://www.pgatour.com/
This website offers a large selection of articles and includes the Official World Golf Ranking.

Official Website for Tiger Woods
http://www.tigerwoods.com
The official website for Tiger Woods contains a newsletter, archives, and videos on the famous golf player.

Tiger Woods Foundation
> http://www.tigerwoodsfoundation.org/
> This website has information on the Tiger Woods Foundation and its
> mission: to help young people achieve their dreams.

Tiger Woods Learning Center
> http://www.twlc.org/
> The Tiger Woods Learning Center helps students plan for the future
> with classes about careers in math, science, technology, and language
> arts.

Video

Tiger Woods PGA Tour 08. Videogame. Redwood City, CA: EA Sports, 2008.
> With an ESRB rating of E for everyone, this game lets you pit yourself
> against Tiger and other PGA or LPGA players.

PHOTO ACKNOWLEDGMENTS

Additional images in this book are used with the permission of: © Stephen Dunn/Getty Images, p. 3; © David Strick/Redux, pp. 4, 12, 14, 20, 21; © Ken Levine/Getty Images, p. 5; © Bettmann/CORBIS, p. 7; © Pierre Barbier/Roger Viollet/Getty Images, p. 9; © Bob Thomas/Bob Thomas Sports Photography/ Getty Images, p. 16 (top left); AP Photo, p. 16 (bottom left); AP Photo/ Lennox McLendon, pp. 16 (top right), 48; San Diego Union-Tribune/Dave Siccardi, p. 22; © Christina Salvador/Sygma/CORBIS, p. 24; © Tony Roberts/ CORBIS, p. 26; © Duomo/CORBIS, pp. 29, 63; © Scott Linnett/San Diego Union Tribune/ZUMA Press, p. 31; © David Madison/NewSport/CORBIS, pp. 35, 62; © J.D. Cuban/Getty Images, pp. 38, 44; AP Photo/Matt York, p. 39; AP Photo/Peter Zuzga, p. 47; AP Photo/Kathy Willens, p. 49; © Todd Strand/Independent Picture Service, p. 51 (top left); © Stephen Munday/ Getty Images, pp. 52, 70 (right); AP Photo/Dave Martin, p. 55; AP Photo/ Amy Sancetta, p. 56; © Craig Jones/Getty Images, p. 59; AP Photo/Dom Furore, Golf Digest, p. 60; AP Photo/Phil Sandlin, p. 64; AP Photo/Kevork Djansezian, p. 66; © Jonathan Ferrey/Getty Images, p. 67; © Brian Spurlock/ USP/ZUMA Press, p. 70 (left); © Susan M. Ogrocki/ZUMA Press, p. 72; © Timothy A. Clary/AFP/Getty Images, p. 78; AP Photo/Paul Sakuma, p. 83; AP Photo/Gregory Bull, p. 84; © John Cordes/USP/ZUMA Press, p. 85; © Harry How/Getty Images, p. 87; AP Photo/Branimir Kvartuc, p. 90; AP Photo/Chris Carlson, p. 93; AP Photo/Damian Dovarganes, p. 96.

Front Cover: © David Cannon/Getty Images.

ABOUT THE AUTHOR

Jeremy Roberts is the pen name of Jim DeFelice. He is also the author of *The Beatles*, *Benito Mussolini*, and *Saint Joan of Arc*, among others. Mr. Roberts has written books about skydiving and rock climbing and wrote a historical trilogy as well as several techno-thrillers. He lives with his wife and son in a haunted farmhouse in Chester, New York.

JAN 1 4 2009

CHESTERFIELD COUNTY LIBRARY
BON AIR